the pop classic series

#1 *It Doesn't Suck.*

Showgirls

#2 *Raise Some Shell.*

Teenage Mutant Ninja Turtles

raise
some shell.
teenage
mutant
ninja turtles
richard
rosenbaum

ecwpress

Copyright © Richard Rosenbaum, 2014

Published by ECW Press
2120 Queen Street East, Suite 200,
Toronto, Ontario, Canada M4E 1E2
416-694-3348 / info@ecwpress.com

Printing: Webcom 5 4 3 2 1

Library and Archives Canada
Cataloguing in Publication

Rosenbaum, Richard, 1979–, author
Raise some shell : Teenage Mutant Ninja
Turtles / Richard Rosenbaum.

(Pop classics ; 2)
Includes bibliographical references.
Issued in print and electronic formats.
ISBN 978-1-77041-179-1 (pbk.)
Also issued as: 978-1-77090-521-4 (pdf);
978-1-77090-522-1 (epub)

1. Teenage Mutant Ninja Turtles (Fictitious
characters)–Social aspects. I. Title.

PN6728.T35R68
2014 741.5'973 C2013-908024-4
C2013-908025-2

Editors for the press:
Crissy Calhoun and Jennifer Knoch
Cover and text design: David Gee

The publication of *Raise Some Shell* has been generously supported by the Canada Council
for the Arts, which last year invested $157 million to bring the arts to Canadians throughout
the country, and by the Ontario Arts Council (OAC), an agency of the Government of Ontario,
which last year funded 1,681 individual artists and 1,125 organizations in 216 communities
across Ontario for a total of $52.8 million. We also acknowledge the financial support of the
Government of Canada through the Canada Book Fund for our publishing activities, and the
contribution of the Government of Ontario through the Ontario Book Publishing Tax Credit and
the Ontario Media Development Corporation.

Ontario
Ontario Media Development
Corporation

ONTARIO ARTS COUNCIL
CONSEIL DES ARTS DE L'ONTARIO
50 YEARS OF ONTARIO GOVERNMENT SUPPORT OF THE ARTS
50 ANS DE SOUTIEN DU GOUVERNEMENT DE L'ONTARIO AUX ARTS

Canada Council
for the Arts

Conseil des Arts
du Canada

Canadä

MIX
Paper from
responsible sources
FSC® C004071

Contents

Introduction: TMNT & Me   ix

Origins and Evolutions   1

Coming Out of Their Shells   22

The Rise and Fall of Turtle Power   52

Remixed and Reincarnated   100

Turtles All the Way Down   116

Notes   131

Acknowledgments   133

"My soul is wrought to sing of forms transformed to bodies new and strange!"

— Ovid, *Metamorphoses*

Introduction: TMNT & Me

Depending on how you look at it, the Teenage Mutant Ninja Turtles began life either in a puddle of phosphorescent sludge under the mean streets of New York (back when those streets really *were* mean, before Giuliani's reign) or in a cramped apartment that dreamed of being an artist's studio in Dover, New Hampshire. In the following years, TMNT evolved into the most successful independent comic book ever, the world's most fearsome fighting team, a global phenomenon, the best new reason to order a pizza and learn self-defense, and a precedent-setting transmedia franchise never before seen in the annals of pop culture history.

Ninja Turtles inspired countless imitators, numerous detractors, and fanatical devotion from people of all ages and backgrounds. They fought against street gangs in filthy alleys, hid underground by day, and ran and jumped across the rooftops by night, shouting catchphrases and jokes. They drove without a license, traveled through time and across dimensions, drank underage in extraterrestrial dive bars, and saved humanity from the forces of evil hundreds upon hundreds of times.

In their own world (or should that be *worlds?*), they kept to the shadows as proper ninjas are wont to do, their good deeds perpetually unsung. But in our world — gosh, we loved them, didn't we? I, for one, still do. There's a good chance that you do too. After 30 years (and counting) of the Turtles, not only are we not bored of them, but new generations of fans are even today discovering Leonardo, Michelangelo, Donatello, and Raphael for the first time.

Ninja Turtles clearly touches something deep and important in our culture. But why? Why the massive success, and why the tireless longevity? Why do we still remember and still care about the Turtles? What is it about them, and about us, that makes these stories resonate so strongly?

I was in fourth grade when I discovered the Turtles; I was nine or ten, and it must have been 1989. *Fraggle Rock* had been over for two years; *He-Man* for four. To a little kid, these expired obsessions were by then like vivid dreams from a previous life. I'd moved on to building Proton Packs out of paper-towel rolls and ghost traps from Kleenex boxes and flying through the future and past with my cardboard-and-magic-marker DeLorean.

It was in art class, I think, that some kid brought out one of his action figures — I don't remember exactly which one it was, but let's say it was Donatello because he is clearly and objectively the best.[1] I didn't recognize it, this weird, muscly, anthropomorphic reptile wearing a bandana and a toothy scowl, so I asked the kid what it was from. He said, "*Ninja Turtles*."

My follow-up question: "When is it on?"

Now I don't have a clear memory of first watching the show, but I do know it made an immediate and unmistakable impression on me, because the following fall when I caught chicken pox and had to stay home from school for two weeks of unavailing, pustular torment, and my mom kindly asked what she could do to make me feel better, I said, "Buy me a Ninja Turtles comic."

Which she did. It was *Teenage Mutant Ninja Turtles Adventures* #13. I didn't know it at the time, but this wasn't the comic series that had kicked off the whole Turtle craze. It was from the series published by Archie Comics, which retold stories from the cartoon for its first four issues but then veered off into its own new parallel dimension of original content. What I did know was this wasn't the TMNT from my Saturday morning and weekday afternoon pilgrimages to the altar of television. They were the same four Turtles, sure — though Raphael was, for some unexplained reason, wearing a full-body black suit like the one Spider-Man had been sporting the last few years — but I'd been dropped into a whole different universe. The Turtles were stranded on an alien planet called Hirobyl, apparently carried there inside the mouth of

---

1 Everyone has a favorite Turtle, of course, just like everyone has a favorite Beatle. So if you happen to prefer Raphael's intractable intensity, or Michelangelo's gregarious charm, or if you count yourself among the proud few Leonardo lovers . . . well, you're wrong, sorry. Donatello for the win.

a bus-sized disembodied cow's head by the name of Cudley the Cowlick, battling an army of insect-men they referred to as Maligna's Children while winged video cameras circled, broadcasting the fight on an extragalactic television channel owned and operated by a pair of talking trees named Stump and Sling. Shredder and Krang, and their lackeys Rocksteady and Bebop, were around, as was the alligator mutant Leatherhead, but there was also some buffed-up, cigar-chomping human called Trap; a giant talking fruitbat and his wisecracking mosquito sidekick, Wingnut and Screwloose (respectively); and a purple-skinned witch named Cherubae, who was being held captive by a group of gray-skinned, pie-eyed aliens she called the Sons of Silence.

I had no idea what was going on.

And it was *awesome*.

Superheroes were not strangers to me. The guts of comic books, covers torn off and lost from rereading after rereading,[2] lived in my drawers: Green Lantern and Superboy; Spider-Man and Power Pack. That stuff could get pretty weird. But this — this whole Turtle thing — was different. It was full of humor but also sincerity. It was brain-meltingly bizarre but still came down, ultimately, to a relatable story: a family sticking together when the odds were against them and important things were at stake. It was something *special* — something that snapped its sharp jaws down hard on my brain and told me in no uncertain terms that it was refusing to ever let go again.

---

2 Before, obviously, I learned about Mylar® comic book sleeves and acid-free backing boards and turned into one of those totally insufferable paranoiacs afraid of my own finger oils.

Nostalgia is big these days. You might have noticed. Everything old is new again, as they say, and anything that made money in the 1980s is currently being recycled, rereleased, repurposed, and rerun for the benefit of the grown-up(ish) versions of the kids who were into the stuff back in the day and now have money to throw away on Build Your Own Optimus Prime Lego sets and faux-faded t-shirts silk-screened with images of Snarf being an idiot. A cynic could easily dismiss the Turtles' resurgence as just another symptom of the profligate hipsteria of our age and leave it at that. But while nostalgia is a part of what's happening, it isn't the whole story. Not only does that explanation not go far enough with respect to the Turtles' perpetual success, but it ignores the ways in which the nostalgia factor is being used in TMNT's contemporary incarnations differently — and better — than its fellow properties use it.

At the zenith of its popularity in the late '80s and early '90s, TMNT was exponentially more successful than any of its competitors, and even when other inferior entertainments arose to usurp the Turtles' rightful place in the spotlight, Ninja Turtles never entirely disappeared from the cultural consciousness. There have only been a few short moments during which TMNT laid completely fallow between its inception in 1984 and today.

Teenage Mutant Ninja Turtles, with its origins in the smudgy gutters of self-publishing, has proven itself to be a cultural force with as much relevance, depth, and cachet as any of the giants that started out with the benefits of Hollywood money and corporate resources. Not despite but because of the versatility designed into their very DNA, the Turtles captivated their audience as the ideal heroes for the fragmented and hybridized times in which we lived and still live, uniquely suited to tell all the different kinds of stories that we wanted and needed to hear. And still do.

1

Origins and Evolutions

The early 1980s saw a radical transformation in the medium of comics. The mainstream was growing darker: writer and artist Frank Miller was drawing Marvel Comics toward the shadows with his run on *Daredevil* (May 1979–February 1983) — blind lawyer by day and superpowered crimefighter by night. Particularly with his creation of the ninja assassin Elektra and his greater focus on issues of corruption, drugs, and organized crime, Miller was at the forefront of the wave of "gritty" titles that surged in popularity over the next decade. At the same time, he published his groundbreaking miniseries *Ronin* (1983–1984), in which an ancient Japanese warrior is reborn in a futuristic New York City and attempts to bring a destructive gang war to an end. *Ronin* heralded a deepening interest in Japanese culture and tradition within American art

— actually influenced by the art coming out of Japan itself. *Ronin*'s largest debt was to the manga series *Lone Wolf and Cub*, and Miller later created original covers for the series when it was eventually published in North America.

Meanwhile, Miller's colleague at Marvel Chris Claremont was carrying the other side of the banner for the avant-garde of mainstream superhero comics. In 1975, he was given writing duties for a second-tier title called *X-Men* and was well on his way to turning it into the bestselling comic book of all time. *X-Men* (and later *The New Mutants*) told stories of a group of superpowered humans born into a world that hated and feared them, who nevertheless fought to protect that world from others born with similar gifts and an overdeveloped sense of entitlement. The depth of Claremont's characterization combined with his strong understanding of how to deploy symbolism and social metaphors struck a chord with readers, and *X-Men* became the model of what a successful comic looked like for the next two decades.

At the time, *Daredevil*, *Ronin*, and *X-Men* were the domain of comics' most brightly shining stars. But in the medium's darker corners lurked a different sort of animal. Specialty comic book stores emerged in the early 1970s (culminating in the formation of Diamond Comic Distributors, which, by the late '90s, had practically monopolized the direct market for comics), creating a new space for family-unfriendly fare, and artists around the world used this channel to find an audience for more serious work in a form that was too often dismissed as kids' stuff. The most notable of these new underground comics was *Cerebus the Aardvark*, created, written, and drawn by cartoonist Dave Sim from Hamilton, Ontario, Canada. *Cerebus* started out as a straight-ahead parody, a comedic mash-up of Marvel's *Howard the Duck* and *Conan the Barbarian* featuring an anthropomorphic aardvark mercenary named Cerebus who adventured through a magical and very anachronistic continent called Estarcion, seeking fortune and . . . well, pretty much just fortune. *Cerebus* proved to be a success against all odds, and Sim became a leading figure in the creator-owned comics movement. *Cerebus* ran for 300 self-published issues (between 1977 and 2004, which Sim convincingly describes as the longest continuous work of narrative in recorded human history); it wandered far from its roots and turned into a deep and controversial meditation on contemporary issues such as politics, religion, and gender — often tackled with humor, and just as often provoking outrage among its readers, or increasingly its ex-readers. Despite its later years, *Cerebus* served as a model and Sim as inspiration for countless other artists who wished to work in the medium of comics but whose subject matter was either not commercial enough or too antisocial for the mainstream publishers.

By the time 1984 rolled around, most comics fans were reading about teenage mutants like the X-Men, ninjas like Daredevil and his foes, and funny animals such as Cerebus the Aardvark.

Enter Kevin Eastman and Peter Laird.

Artists and friends, Eastman and Laird were plainly obsessed with the work of Frank Miller and Dave Sim, as well as that of Jack "The King" Kirby, who co-created most of the Marvel Universe in the 1960s and was known for the powerful fluidity of his action sequences, which cemented the visual grammar for superhero comics forever after. Eastman and Laird wanted to make their own mark on the world of comics, and they'd seen some small successes. One evening, Kevin Eastman, in an attempt to irritate Peter Laird while he watched television (as is every good roommate's wont), sketched a turtle standing upright with a pair of nunchucks strapped to its arms and the words "NINJA TURTLE" written above it. Laird looked at the drawing and laughed, redrew it in his own style, added the words "TEENAGE MUTANT," and handed the page back to Eastman. The two of them knew that they had something. They didn't know quite what yet, but it was something they'd created together that made them laugh, and as they refined the idea — eventually creating four Turtles, each wielding a different weapon — they grew fascinated with the concept. They decided to delve into the world of these Turtles: who they were, where they came from, what they were all about. *Teenage Mutant Ninja Turtles* #1 was a 40-page black-and-white martial-arts science-fiction story; guided by *Ronin* stylistically and by *Cerebus* in terms of its non-corporate, do-it-yourself production process, the book was financed with tax returns and a loan from Eastman's uncle. They printed only 3,000 copies in a weird, magazine-style oversized edition (because the printer they hired had never done or apparently even seen a comic book before) and debuted it at a local comic convention in the spring of 1984.

The book sold out in less time than it took to pronounce its hilariously unwieldy title. The Turtles phenomenon had officially begun.

The name of the game: *pastiche*. Pastiche is a literary technique where an author takes the major tropes from one or more existent works and uses them to create something new. Pastiche can be limited to a single passing reference, can overrun an entire work from beginning to end, or fall anywhere between the two extremes. When pastiche is used primarily to highlight the weaknesses of the original work in a comedic way, either affectionately or derisively or both, that's parody or satire. When done poorly, pastiche can be little more than barely concealed plagiarism, by artists who are either not talented enough to come up with anything original or so cynical that they think they can cash in on the success of something that's currently popular — or both. In the parlance of literary/cultural theory, that's called a *ripoff*.[3] The third major form of pastiche is *homage*, and it tends to be used to call attention to the tropes it's co-opting, sometimes by explicitly subverting them.[4]

_____

3 At least in polite company. If the theorist in question has had a couple of drinks, you may also hear this type of pastiche referred to as *total bullshit*.

4 The borders between these three categories are fairly permeable, so don't concern yourself overmuch with slotting specific works solely under one heading. But just to give you some concrete examples, let's take horror movies. *Scream* is a parody. *The Cabin in the Woods* is homage, as is *Shaun of the Dead* — the latter is one of those borderline cases, because it's not making fun of horror movies as such; it plays most of the traditional horror tropes completely straight, it just sticks lots of jokes in between them. *The Village* is total bullshit.

A pastiche works best when the audience doesn't need to be familiar with the works being referenced in order to enjoy it. So, for instance, you can dig *Star Wars* without ever having heard of *Flash Gordon*, even though the former is heavily indebted to the latter. If a work is influential enough that it inspires a large number of different artists to pastiche it, it can lead to the creation of a whole new form; imitators of Edgar Allan Poe evolved the mystery genre, and J.R.R. Tolkien's thralls propagated high fantasy.

At the far abstract end of pastiche, a creator appropriates the structure of one or more works but empties out the content and fills it with their own. The effect of this is twofold. First, if it works at all, it tends to work really well: because the content is original, it doesn't rely exclusively on the works it's referencing for its success. It's enjoyable on its own merits because the parts that are borrowed are below the surface and not necessarily immediately apparent. The skeleton may be stolen, but the flesh is fresh.

Second, this application of pastiche is particularly suitable for purposes of deconstruction, which is why it's been so popular in postmodern art. Postmodernism is interested to the point of obsession in constructedness and in reexamining past works to expose the architecture of their influences, assumptions, and internal contradictions; their successes and, especially, their failures. A lot (though certainly not all) of postmodern art is content to vivisect the canon with its audience sitting in the operating theater and then go home, leaving it out to die on the surgeon's table.[5] Beckett, Pynchon, and a lot of Brett Easton Ellis's stuff tend to fall into this category, exposing the emptiness without any suggestion for how to fix the situations, implying an inevitable hopelessness.

Art — in my opinion, better art — can do more than deconstruct; it can *reconstruct*. It can take a work apart, even strip it down to its bones, and then proceed to sew to it a new skin made of insight and love for its source materials.

And this is the genius of Teenage Mutant Ninja Turtles.

The transformations occurring in comics in the mid '80s that grabbed the imagination of readers, among them Eastman and Laird, were very much on the surface of the medium, in its stories and its visuals, but still only half-formed, at an experimental stage of finding itself. It would be a couple more years before two DC superhero miniseries solidified the tropes by powerfully deconstructing them: *The Dark Knight Returns*, Frank Miller's, again, with a brutally dark take on the future of Batman, and, simultaneously, *Watchmen* by the English writer Alan Moore.[6] Growing dominant at this time were a number

---

5 Because postmodernists are sociopaths.

6 Noteworthy are the divergent paths that these two comics heavyweights personally took after their accidental partnership in reshaping the medium: Miller has grown politically conservative (coincidentally or not, he lived in New York City's Hell's Kitchen on September 11, 2001, about four miles from the World Trade Center) and used his comics and blog to espouse his anti-left views. Alan Moore has gone in the opposite direction, adopting political anarchism and the practice of ceremonial magic and devoting himself to the Ancient Greek snake god Glycon, who Moore himself openly admits was probably just a hand puppet (no, but *seriously*). The third father of that era, Dave Sim, has also since had a pretty significant personal transformation and converted to an idiosyncratic non-denominational monotheism, and the content of *Cerebus* turned heavily theological. The latter days of *Cerebus* have, I think, been unfairly criticized by people who take Sim's philosophy way too personally, which has also happened with much of Miller's and Moore's later works. Kevin Eastman and Peter Laird, I should mention, have both remained pretty normal.

of tropes bleaker than had been typical in superhero comics. The seeds of evil being sown by the hero's attempts to do good, resulting in an unwinnable cycle of destruction. Good guys and bad guys not being significantly far apart in either their motivations or, often, their tactics. The implicit condescension-bordering-on-fascism of self-proclaimed heroes' vigilantism. Contradictions inherent in the moral systems of superheroes who always considered themselves above the law when it came to fighting their personal enemies.

There was a new seriousness in superhero comics, but at the same time a lot of what was going on was pretty ridiculous and hacky. Daredevil was created to be a darker and more adult version of Spider-Man; Matt Murdock lived just a few subway stops away from Peter Parker, and the distance between suspension of disbelief and straight-up cognitive dissonance was equally small when you read those early Miller *DD* stories. We're still talking about a dude with radar who dresses up like a demon to fight ninjas in midtown Manhattan, after all. *TMNT* would crank up the ridiculosity to ten but play the whole thing totally straight; so it was hilariously absurd and yet totally super badass at the same time. And by wearing its influences openly and proudly, it declared exactly what it was trying to do — comment on contemporary genre trends — while never ever condescending to its audience or disrespecting its heroes.

That first issue of *TMNT* (May 1984) wanted so much to connect itself to what it was pastiching that Eastman and Laird made the Turtles' origin a direct result of Daredevil's. In *Daredevil* #1, we meet the young Matthew Murdock, son of the professional boxer "Battlin' Jack" Murdock. One day Matt sees a blind man crossing the street about to be struck by an out-of-control transport truck. Matt leaps into the street to push the blind man out of the truck's path. As the truck driver swerves, a canister of nuclear material flies from the truck and hits Matt in the face. The nuclear radiation blinds him but causes his other senses to become superhumanly heightened and gives him a radar-like sense that allows him to become the superhero Daredevil.

In *TMNT* #1, we witness the same event, but instead of following Matthew Murdock, we follow the path of the canister. After striking the young hero near his eyes, the canister bounces, smashing a glass bowl containing four baby turtles that had just been purchased by a bystander to the incident. The turtles and the canister fall into an open manhole. Landing in the sewer, the canister breaks, and the turtles — as well as a rat with an already elaborate backstory of his own — are doused in mysterious glowing ooze. It causes them to mutate into the Turtles we all know and love.

The pastiche goes even further than that. In Miller's *Daredevil*, the deadly ninja clan that becomes the character's primary opposition is known as the Hand. In *TMNT*, the Turtles are sent to eliminate the Shredder, leader of a deadly ninja clan called the Foot. The enigmatic ninja master who first trained Matt Murdock in the acrobatics and fighting techniques he uses as a superhero is named Stick. So, of course, the wizened mutant rat who serves as father figure and sensei to the Turtles is named Splinter.

A great portion of the visual and structural elements of that first issue of *Ninja Turtles* is torn, blatantly and unapologetically, from the pages of Miller's *Ronin*. Action panels are lifted nearly wholesale, with mutant turtles drawn in place of the reincarnated masterless samurai. Right down to the jagged panel borders and even the title font, reading early issues of *TMNT* is like watching a toddler imitate the mannerisms of its beloved parent, and the effect is a similar mix of captivating and adorable.

There's an oblique allusion to this imitation in Splinter's tale of his own origin: he was once an ordinary rat, the pet of the world-class ninja master Hamato Yoshi. From inside his cage, Splinter learned the most advanced techniques by watching and imitating Yoshi's moves as he practiced every day for years. Splinter says that, at the time, Yoshi was amused to see his pet rat playing at being a ninja, and nobody ever mentions that this is insanely humanlike behavior for an animal that wouldn't be exposed to the DNA-transforming mutagen until many years later. Similarly, Splinter explains that he chose names for the Turtles from a battered book about Renaissance art that he found in a storm drain — *but how the hell did he learn to read?* Later incarnations of *TMNT* would solve the mystery by making Splinter the mutated form of Hamato Yoshi himself, but in the original comic, these weren't problems at all. They were winks at the very canny audience: Frank Miller was the Master, and Eastman and Laird just a matted fuzzball absorbing his techniques and emulating his movements as best they could.

As you can see, the pastiche is strong in this one.

The first few *TMNT* books provide a wealth of insight on the inborn intertextuality of the Turtles' world and the characters themselves. Early in the second issue, we actually see issues of *Ronin* and *Cerebus* splayed out on the floor of the Turtles' sewer lair.[7]

The point being that *Teenage Mutant Ninja Turtles* was not a dumb parody of the popular comics of the time; it was an extremely smart pastiche by a pair of very talented artists, written for people just like themselves. Those who loved what Frank Miller and Dave Sim were proving was possible in a medium commonly regarded as trash, but who could also recognize and revel in the absurdity and contradictions inherent in taking Jack Kirby–style B-movie action tropes and treating them as literature, rather than empty entertainment made to kill time. It was a perfect confluence of beautiful art, sharp storytelling, engaging characterization, and a pair of minds thick with inspiration from which to draw, and that's why it succeeded. To the readers who were in on the joke, the fellow Frank Miller fans who knew exactly what the Turtles' creators were doing, there were laughs of recognition to be had on pretty much every page. For others, the book was strong

---

7 The *Cerebus* comic's appearance is especially weird in hindsight: the Turtles would go on to meet the eponymous aardvark in issue #8. But its presence speaks to Eastman and Laird's pride in their influences. If you're interested, the books on display on the Turtles' shelf on that same page are: *The Book of Five Rings* by Miyamoto Musashi, a 17th-century Japanese philosophical and martial arts treatise; H.W. Janson's *History of Art*; Bruce Lee's *Tao of Jeet Kune Do*; *The World Encyclopedia of Cartoons* by Maurice Horn; *The Enormous Egg* by Oliver Butterworth, a classic children's book in which a chicken lays the titular enormous egg from which hatches a baby triceratops; *The Way Things Work* by David Macaulay, an introduction to science and technology for children; the *Complete Works of William Shakespeare*; *History of Games*; *Care and Keeping of Your Turtle*; and something by Pascal, the complete title of which is obscured. I've had some fun speculating which books belonged to which Turtle, and which to Splinter. Leo is reading Frank Herbert's *Dune* in this panel.

enough on its own to be compelling — the story of four brothers shunned by society, determined to exact vengeance on the man who shattered their father's family.[8] The book's appeal was multidimensional and so were its fans — the art and its audience drew strength from one another, rather than pulling the Turtles' paradoxes apart, because *they got it*.

Strengthening the pastiche was the fact that Teenage Mutant Ninja Turtles was subversive.

On one level, the whole creator-owned, self-publishing thing was a protest against the stifling hegemony of mainstream comics. It's true that Marvel was putting out Miller's groundbreaking *Daredevil* stuff, and DC would do Alan Moore's masterpiece *Watchmen* a couple of years later, but the sorts of contracts that the Big Two publishers were giving to writers and artists were overwhelmingly work-for-hire. Anything created or worked on while employed by the publisher was the property of the publisher rather than the creator. So, for instance, Frank Miller had created, in the pages of *Daredevil*, the extremely popular character of Elektra, Matt Murdock's onetime love and deadliest foe. But Elektra did not belong to Miller; according to contract, she belonged to Marvel. When Miller stopped working on *Daredevil*, Marvel was free to give the character to somebody else and let them

---

8 In his book *The Anxiety of Influence*, literary critic Harold Bloom calls this kind of thing "strong misreading," where an author, in the attempt to master the style of their predecessors, creates meaning that could not exist without it and produces an excess or overflow that brings about a condition of newness. This is the process by which literature evolves.

do whatever they wanted with it, regardless of how Miller felt. Same thing with Alan Moore and everything he did for DC with *Swamp Thing* and others. This is why DC can still put out a prequel series called *Before Watchmen* and Moore can't do anything to stop them. Alan Moore became so outraged and disappointed in what DC had done with what he considered his intellectual property that he refused to have his name on any derivative works (he especially hates the movie adaptations), and he gives any royalties from said derivative works to the artist who worked on the book in question.[9]

So the late 1970s and early 1980s saw an explosion of advocacy for creator's rights. Jack Kirby was so pissed off at how he'd been treated by Marvel that he quit, and Miller and Moore were a couple of his most outspoken advocates. *Ninja Turtles* emerged into the era's burgeoning indie comics scene, and Eastman and Laird (along with Dave Sim and others) would be some of the first signatories to the Creator's Bill of Rights that outlined the expectation that comics creators had the right to own and control their own creations and be remunerated fairly for their work.

In terms of content too, Eastman and Laird were deconstructing the deconstructions in which comics were currently delighting: the Turtles as characters were drawn in stark moral opposition to what was popular in both mainstream and underground comics at the time.

The Manichean good-versus-evil of earlier superhero

---

9 Let's not even get started on the copyright clusterfuck that is *Miracleman*.

comics was on its way to being hopelessly muddied, mostly thanks to Frank Miller. It wasn't just the tone of the stories that was getting darker; the moral decisions that our heroes faced were growing less black and white as well. Daredevil behaved more and more questionably to accomplish his goals by employing violence, which his (ironically pacifist) boxer father, his inspiration for becoming a crime-fighter, would have abhorred. Across the hall at *X-Men*, the Canadian mutant antihero Wolverine was slashing berserkly through the flesh of his foes on his way to becoming the undisputed economic engine of superhero comics. And *The Punisher* was darker still: a former Green Beret and Vietnam vet (this was all happening in the late '70s, remember, and the wounds of Vietnam in the American psyche were not yet fully scabbed over) returns home to find that his family has been murdered by gangsters. He devotes the rest of his life to hunting down and personally executing not only those who killed his wife and children but anyone he considers to be a criminal.

When *The Dark Knight Returns* rolled out in 1986, Frank Miller made us wonder who was crazier — the Clown Prince of Crime or the Caped Crusader himself? Alan Moore's *Watchmen* was the final nail in that particular coffin, where the heroes are mostly racist, misogynistic, abusive murderers,[10] and the bad guy wins, orchestrating a fake alien invasion that claims the lives of about four million innocent people, forcing

---

10 To be fair, one of them is only an amoral, affectless inhuman.

the human race to unite against the "threat," thereby ending the Cold War and ultimately bringing world peace.[11]

Also at DC, Lobo emerged. A Superman villain, originally an over-the-top parody of the grim and gritty antiheroes like Wolverine and the Punisher that were ascendant at the time, Lobo became a star in his own right; as Lobo's popularity transcended the irony that had gone into his character, he more or less became what he had been created to satirize. To give you a sense of Lobo, his origin story is that he's the last surviving member of an alien race called the Czarnians. Why is Lobo the Last Czarnian? He created a plague to wipe out every other member of his race for no particular reason.

In indie comics, things were not any better. Cerebus the Aardvark was an egomaniacal, foul-tempered, alcoholic mercenary who at one point, while he briefly held the title of Pope of the Eastern Church of Tarim, threw a baby off the front steps of the Regency Hotel.[12] Cerebus was so out of control that Dave Sim himself broke the fourth wall, interceding directly to tell the aardvark that he seriously ought to chill out.

It's not like the Turtles didn't kill people. The Turtles killed people. The Turtles killed a *lot* of people. The very first scene in *TMNT* has the Turtles ninja-ing to death 15 members of the Purple Dragons, the toughest street gang on the East Side. But the Turtles didn't start that fight. At the end of that first issue, when they've taken out countless Foot ninjas and

---

11 It makes sense in context.

12 This also makes sense in context. He was trying to prove a point. It's played for laughs.

bested the evil Shredder himself, who was responsible for the cold-blooded murder of Splinter's master, Hamato Yoshi, the Turtles give Shredder a way out. They offer him the opportunity to commit *seppuku*, ritual suicide, and thus exit this life with some semblance of honor. Shredder, of course, declines and instead produces a thermite grenade. He intends to detonate the rooftop on which they're fighting and destroy the Turtles along with himself. Thinking fast, Donatello launches his bo staff at Shredder, knocking him off the side of the building. Shredder lands in a dumpster, which (because of the activated grenade in his hand) promptly explodes.[13]

Ninjas are not known for their adherence to honor codes. The samurai were eminently honorable; the specialties of the ninja were sabotage, espionage, and assassination. Yet the Ninja Turtles did not sneak up behind Shredder and murder him; they invited him out into open combat and put their own lives at risk of his treachery to afford him a chance to retain some semblance of dignity. Not only were the Turtles atypical superheroes for their era — displaying compassion and tolerance more common in an earlier, more innocent age of comic books, an age that the establishment was trying its hardest to escape — they were atypical ninjas.

The Turtles were subversive in other ways as well. They are, if you think about it, the ultimate superheroes of the subaltern (a group that's inherently excluded from society's dominant power structure). Look at their contemporaries

---

13 Donnie is the best.

and what you'll see, almost exclusively, is a pack of privileged white guys.

Bruce Wayne? Inherited billions of dollars from his parents — his father, Thomas Wayne, was a world-renowned physician, plus the heir to a fortune his father and grandfather had amassed through heavy industry and real estate; his mother, Martha Wayne (née Kane), was a lifelong philanthropist and patroness of the arts, which she funded with the fortune that she inherited from her father's chemical manufacturing company. Bruce is old money on both sides of his family. He never had to work a day in his life.

Tony Stark? Also a billionaire, thanks to his father's multinational corporation that has supplied weapons and defense technology to the United States government for decades. Tony inherited Stark Industries when his parents died in a plane crash, but Howard Stark inherited it from his own father, its founder Isaac Stark, so Tony is a third-generation billionaire just like Bruce Wayne. Tony is also a super-genius who was accepted to MIT to study electrical engineering at age 15. He's physically attractive and charismatic, with no trouble finding a date for Saturday night if he wants one.

Peter Parker? Genius-level intelligence, university educated, photographer for a major metropolitan newspaper. Was married to a supermodel. Enjoys enough middle-class economic stability to keep an apartment in Manhattan.

Matt Murdock? Yes, he's blind, but he also earned his J.D.

from Columbia Law School and became the most successful and famous criminal defense attorney in America.

Even the X-Men, who profess that the world hates and fears them, are students at an exclusive private school in Westchester, New York — one of the wealthiest counties in the United States, home to America's most coveted suburban communities. You'd need to be in possession of some pretty compromising photos of the governor just to rent a shitty basement apartment down the street from the X-Men's place (known colloquially as the X-Mansion).

These guys are all heroes *because they can afford to be*. Any of them could be doing something else. They all have regular lives that would be enviable even without the costumes and superpowers. Sure, most of their parents are dead, and that sucks, but being an orphan doesn't automatically make you a hero. Instead of stalking the night to wreak vengeance on the criminal element or assuage his guilty conscience, Bruce Wayne could spend a tenth of his monthly batarang budget on a good therapist. The vast majority of superheroes really could get along perfectly well in regular human society if they wanted to. Most of the X-Men could, if they chose to, just stay in the mutant closet. The Justice League headquarters is practically a country club — an ivory tower full of upper-class, attractive, Caucasian trust-fund kids talking politics. Token woman. Token Martian.

Not the Turtles though.

The Teenage Mutant Ninja Turtles have never had the

luxury of hiding behind secret identities. The fact that they are *human-sized turtles* bars them from the regular-lives-by-day-and-heroes-at-night approach of their mainstream counterparts. Even if Bruce Wayne is only a mask that Batman wears, it is a very convincing one. Tony Stark may be open about the fact that he is Iron Man, but he also has the force of his mind-boggling wealth plus the rest of the superhero community to act as a shield against the consequences of that knowledge being public. The Turtles have no material wealth, no social status whatsoever. They are trapped between the human world and the animal world, unable to fit in either one. They have no one but each other and their adoptive father, Splinter, another hybrid, and himself exiled twice over — losing first his home and then the only family he ever knew. Even when the Turtles expand their sphere to include a few others — humans such as April O'Neil and Casey Jones, or other mutants stuck between worlds — this community is always inherently smaller, and yet more fractured, than any comparable human subculture. The Turtles and Splinter are a subculture unto themselves — a *sub* culture in the most literal sense, as they actually live in the sewers below the multicultural landscape of New York City.

And their moral code prevents them from trying to usurp power for themselves. They never seek acceptance from human civilization, but they do protect it. In *X-Men*, Magneto serves as the Malcolm X analog to Professor Xavier's Martin Luther King Jr. — the former intends to overthrow the unfair power structures of civilization using violence, while the latter intends to enfranchise oppressed mutants by raising political consciousness. The mainstream mutants of Marvel — heroes and villains alike — of which the TMNT were a deliberate pastiche are all very concerned with overturning the dominant power structures to benefit their own group. But the Turtles have no interest in power or in a revolution. They sometimes resent their position (or non-position) in society, but they do understand it. Like Professor Xavier, they attribute this oppression to ignorance rather than malice, but they lack both the numbers and the resources to do anything about it. They can't start a fancy boarding school or hire lobbyists to grease pockets of elected representatives to speak out in favor of mutant rights. But they don't use that as an excuse to be passive. Their deeply ingrained moral code forces them to act. *They never give up*, but they don't seek enfranchisement by overturning the status quo. As a matter of fact, in the Turtles' world, transforming society by force (whether with violence or science) is strictly the modus operandi of the bad guys.

The Turtles are a single family, at once apart from the world and for it, at the vertex of every imaginable opposing idea of identity. And it's this almost paradoxical combination — their total inherent and even irrevocable Otherness plus their belief in timeless and objective notions of right and wrong — that makes them so incredibly compelling as characters. The Turtles are heroes not because they want to be, but because they have to be; they *can't not be*. Without wealth, status, or membership in a large-enough group to create social force, there's literally nothing else in this world that the four of them could do that's consistent with their morality. This trope is illustrated beautifully in a short exchange that occurs in the first season of the original *TMNT* cartoon, the first mass-media adaptation of Eastman and Laird's comic that was soon to remodel the world in some totally unpredictable ways:

DONATELLO
But us — turtles — outcasts of society. Why do we have to stand alone against the forces of evil?

MICHELANGELO
Face it, man — it's the only job we're qualified for.

2

Coming Out of Their Shells

By its very nature, pastiche is a hybrid form. But by making hybridity and transformation its subject as well as its structure, *TMNT* was exceptionally well suited to interrogate its primary theme: the issue of multiple identities. It is this perfect parallel of model and motif that makes it especially flexible. Because of the way Ninja Turtles is structured, inside the fictional world but also outside of it, the characters can be used in virtually any kind of story or with any range of tone.

Take, for example, the 1985 Palladium Books tabletop role-playing game based on the original *TMNT* comic, called Teenage Mutant Ninja Turtles & Other Strangeness. Think Dungeons & Dragons but with mutant animals instead of elves or dwarves, and high-tech weaponry instead of magical swords. The game expanded on the world of the comics, and while you could play as any of the Turtles or Splinter, the sourcebook also included rules for creating your own mutant animal characters and instructions for how to play out your own interactive stories based in the Turtles' universe.[14] It was very much in the spirit of adaptation and self-publishing, letting players customize their characters and do whatever they wanted with them, against the backdrop of well-defined rules that the Game Master could alter or discard as he or she saw fit.

This amazing versatility of the Turtles is also what propelled its arguably most commercially successful adaptation to date, the cartoon produced by Ireland-based Murakami-Wolf-Swenson[15] that ran ten seasons, from December 1987 to November 1996. The story of how the very gritty and adult black-and-white indie comic metamorphosed into an animated TV show for kids is an interesting one in itself. It's no secret that kids shows, especially in the '80s, were mostly not much more than half-hour toy commercials. *TMNT* was too, but there were differences that made it unique among its Saturday morning brethren. Playmates Toys was looking for an action figure line that could do battle with its rivals, including Hasbro (G.I. Joe, Transformers) and Mattel (Masters of the Universe). They came upon *Teenage Mutant Ninja Turtles* and thought it could be a hit. Cartoons like *Transformers* and *He-Man and*

---

14 What I most strongly remember from the game was the system whereby your character gained skills by spending experience points, which you earned by performing tasks; meaning that you could, say, do ten backflips to learn Japanese. Which we all thought would be a pretty neat way to live.

15 The company also, weirdly, co-produced the first film Woody Allen ever directed, 1966's pastiche-heavy *What's Up, Tiger Lily?*.

the Masters of the Universe were literally toy commercials — the properties were created by the toy companies, which then paid to produce cartoons that would serve as advertisements for the action figure lines. What Playmates did was *license* the property from its creators, Eastman and Laird, who refused to sell their creation outright. This act was an early victory for the good guys in the creator's rights movement, in which Eastman and Laird became increasingly involved. Although the cartoon itself was owned by the production company (giving Mirage Studios, the indie comics publisher started by Eastman and Laird, only a token amount of creative control), the artists retained all copyright over the characters, meaning that Playmates and Murakami-Wolf-Swenson could never cut them out of the action.

The original Turtles comics were very much *not* for kids, and this was still a couple of years before *The Simpsons* single-handedly broke the medium out of that Animation Age Ghetto that dictated cartoons could not be for adults. To be appropriate for the target demographic — i.e., the little ones who would watch the show and then demand that their parents drive them to Toys "R" Us — some things had to change. It's easy to claim that this was a kind of dumbing down or selling out of the characters, but the reason the show succeeded — and the reason that the multifarious subsequent adaptations would also succeed (with a couple notable exceptions) — is twofold.

First, while the violence was drastically reduced and eclipsed by the humor, the cartoon never wandered so far from its roots that it became unrecognizable; the core of the characters and their relationships, and most importantly the themes and tropes that made the Ninja Turtles comic what it was, remained absolutely intact. The cartoon exaggerated some things and moderated others, but the soul of the series was very much made in the pattern of its prototype.

For instance, as previously mentioned, the Turtles' teacher, Splinter, no longer began life as an ordinary rat, like in the original comics. In the comic, Yoshi goes into exile after killing his rival Oroku Nagi; Nagi broke into Yoshi's home and brutally beat Tang Shen, the woman both Yoshi and Nagi loved but who returned only Yoshi's affections. Yoshi, Shen, and their pet, Splinter, moved to New York City, pursued by Nagi's younger brother, Oroku Saki, who had become a ninja master in his own right and was the leader of the American franchise of the Foot clan under the alias "The Shredder." Saki found and killed Yoshi and Shen; Splinter escaped and later mutated.

Not a very kid-friendly story. In the cartoon, the origin story was softened: Yoshi was framed by Oroku Saki for an attempted attack on their visiting sensei and then banished. Yoshi moved to New York where, in his abject poverty, he had to live in the sewers, where he encountered four baby turtles and the mutagen that transformed them all — Splinter the rat began life as Yoshi the ninja master. The bizarre love triangle and the multiple murders were excised but the basic story of Saki's jealousy leading to Yoshi's downfall remained.

In the second issue of the original *TMNT* comic, we and the Turtles are introduced to Baxter Stockman, a scientist who creates thousands of small robots called Mousers, ostensibly to help control New York City's rat problem. But Stockman's diabolical master plan is to commit crimes by remote control; the Mousers break into banks and so on. Stockman's assistant is April O'Neil, an ambitious computer programmer who learns too much about Stockman's plans. He sets the Mousers after her; she escapes into the sewers and is rescued by the Ninja Turtles, eventually becoming their closest and most trusted human friend. In the cartoon, the Mouser story is mostly left intact, except that Baxter Stockman becomes a lackey of the Shredder, who wants to use the Mousers to seek out and destroy Splinter and the Turtles. Stockman himself is changed from a brilliant but egocentric black man in the comic to a bumbling, stereotypical mad scientist, who is also, for whatever reason, white.[16]

April O'Neil, meanwhile, morphed from a computer programmer to a reporter whose courage and professional ambition (she's always going on about how her next story is the one that's sure to win her a Peabody Award) constantly land her in trouble from which her friends the Turtles have to save her. In the first episode of the cartoon, April is investigating a recent rash of high-profile robberies at scientific equipment companies committed by, apparently, ninjas. When a gang of thugs discovers her and attempts to silence her in the name of the Shredder, the Turtles come to her rescue. This sets the tone for April's role in most of the series; her numerous

---

16 Characters who are ethnic minorities in original works are recast as Caucasians in adaptations so frequently that the phenomenon has its own nickname: it's called a race lift.

abductions became something of a running joke, while April from the comics almost never got kidnapped. Cartoon April also became notorious for wearing a low-cut yellow jumpsuit.[17] This probably did not hurt the show's ratings with nearly pubescent boys.

The nature of the mutagen that transformed the Turtles and Splinter itself underwent a transformation when adapted from the page to the screen. In the original comic, the Turtles eventually discover that the anthropomorphizing glowing ooze was a by-product of scientific experimentation by a mysterious company called Techno-Cosmic Research Industries (or T.C.R.I. — initials emblazoned on the side of the shattered canister). T.C.R.I., it turns out, is owned and operated by members of an alien race called the Utroms. The Utroms look like brains with faces and get around via robotic exoskeletons in human shape. The Utroms are not evil; they've been stranded on Earth for decades and are attempting to construct a "transmat" device, a hyperspace teleporter, to return them to their home planet. The mutagen was a waste product of the Utrom's attempts to manufacture organic microchips, and its effect on Splinter and the Turtles was a complete accident.

The cartoon simplified this: instead of a race of brain creatures just trying to get home, we got the evil Krang — a creature from a parallel universe called Dimension X, who had been banished to Earth for his crimes, separated not only from his vast and loyal army of Stone Warriors, but from his very body.

---

17 You're picturing her cleavage right now, aren't you?

Krang resembles the Utroms from the comics, in that he is a giant gross brain. But unlike the Utroms, Krang was not always a brain creature; he once had a body that must have been at least somewhat humanoid, but his body was forcibly taken from him as part of his punishment and exile. The leader of Krang's army, General Traag, recognizes Krang even in his truncated form, and upon seeing his former commander for the first time since the exile, Traag, in obvious shock, remarks, "Lord Krang! What has happened to your body?!" Krang replies, "Don't look at me!" Having Krang be a victim of physical transformation is one of the ways in which the cartoon stayed true to the spirit of comics even while diverging greatly in content.[18]

So the differences are plentiful between the original comic and the cartoon adaptation, and yet at the basic level the story is the same. It still traces its roots to the superhero comics of the early 1980s; and while the humorous elements tend to dominate in the cartoon, the source of the humor is the Turtles' lighthearted attitude and Shredder's frequently comical incompetence. It decidedly isn't a kind of self-aware, ironic humor based on the absurdity of the premise.[19] So while

18 Body image issues abound across the TMNT franchise, in that the way characters look is directly proportional to how well (if at all) they can integrate into society. When humans mutate, they're rarely happy about gaining new powers; instead they're miserable about the social status that they've lost and usually become villains as a result. Even Bebop and Rocksteady, Shredder's hench-mutants in the 1987 TV series, who volunteered for their mutation (from humans into a warthog and rhinoceros, respectively) are very sensitive about their looks post-mutation. The Turtles often use that to their advantage and mock Bebop and Rocksteady for being ugly *all the time*, and the evil mutants do the same in return. What's weird is that these sorts of gibes genuinely seem to hurt Bebop's and Rocksteady's feelings. At one surprisingly tender moment, Bebop confides to Rocksteady that he has tried on numerous occasions to visit his mother, but every time she sees him she runs away screaming.

19 The show did have occasional fourth-wall-breaking jokes, but that was never a driving force for either plot or humor.

the ironic contrast in the comic between the plot's seriousness and the core idea's inherent weirdness is greatly reduced, the cartoon delights in extended bursts of outright comedy.

The description of the cartoon's plot I just gave actually doesn't sound funny at all, and yet if you watch the show it is really pretty funny. While you can argue that the cartoon was a less-than-reverent adaptation of the comic, it's not a *parody* of the comic, just as the comic was not a parody of *Daredevil* or *Ronin*. This is key: that the underpinnings of what made the comic work are modified only to the extent that's necessary to make the cartoon appropriate for its new audience — not changed arbitrarily — and that the architecture of its origins is respected.

The other thing that makes Ninja Turtles so amenable to adaptation is that adaptation itself — in the biological, dictionary-definition sense of an alteration in a living organism that allows it to become better suited to thrive in its environment — is its most basic and primary theme. Teenage Mutant Ninja Turtles is about how to live in a world where you are something strange and new, something different and unprecedented. How to be a person — how to be a hero — when there's never been anything like you before. In this sense, the biological, physical transformations that are all over the place in every version of Teenage Mutant Ninja Turtles symbolize the struggles of growing up with a *hybrid identity*, of not knowing what to do with the feelings of alienation and

Otherness that come along with it and what to hold on to from all the different and even conflicting elements that came together, seemingly for no good reason, to create you.

In this way, TMNT has mutability built into its very DNA, which gives the concept an amazing degree of flexibility when it comes to the stories it's capable of telling and the ways it can be stretched and altered without breaking.

All these ideas — pastiche, hybridity, and transformation; the socially powerless subaltern navigating between the Scylla and Charybdis of mutually hostile identities; coming to terms with being a freak — are deep in the heart of the art and theory of postmodernism, the historical and ideological period during which readers of the comic and viewers of the cartoon were coming of age. Whether they knew it or not, Turtles fans were grappling with these issues in their daily lives, and with TMNT they were engaging in the cultural dialogue that attempted to resolve and synthesize the confusing realities of life in the late 20th century.

Franz Kafka used the symbolism of physical-transformation-as-alienation in his most famous short story, "The Metamorphosis," wherein insurance salesman Gregor Samsa wakes one morning to find himself transformed into an enormous insect. Salman Rushdie too used the exact same trope in his novel *The Satanic Verses*. In that book, two Indian men, nominally Muslim, are on board an airplane flying from India to Britain that is hijacked by Sikh terrorists. The plane explodes, and the two protagonists plunge tens of thousands of feet and land in the English Channel. Miraculously they survive, but they are both changed by the experience — one gains the form of an angel, while the other is reconfigured into a devil. *The Satanic Verses* is about the immigrant experience, of trying to live with a hybrid identity in a world that doesn't yet have the language to conceptualize the kind of thing that you are. You may be glorified as an escapee from a more primitive place or demonized as an immoral alien invader. The book also wrestles with what happens to Grand Narratives in an increasingly intertextual age: both your new home and the old one attempt to claim you or reject you on their own terms, imposing a narrative on your identity in which you may or may not have any interest.

This is also what Ninja Turtles does. It takes all the most pressing issues of identity being faced by citizens of the postmodern age, fuses them together, and presents them in a cool and entertaining way. Kids, maybe even more than adults, were and are dealing with the new kind of people we are supposed to be in Western postmodernity, where ethnic, religious, and political identity — the Grand Narratives that had defined us for all of human history up until now — are melding together into a confusing and unnavigable hot hybrid mess. Worse, kids mostly don't even know they're dealing with this, which could be a big part of the appeal that the Green Team held with the under-12 demographic right from the start.

New York has often been considered the archetype of the postmodern city. While the Mirage comic was set in New York as a reference to Frank Miller's *Daredevil* and *Ronin*, arguably the reason that *they* were set in NYC is the city's persistent use as synecdoche for America (and, to a somewhat lesser extent, the West as a whole). The cartoon, maybe surprisingly, uses the setting as a catalyst for plot more explicitly than in many other versions of TMNT. The cartoon focused on street crime in New York much more than the original comic did, and this spilled into the first movie as well. Crime was often treated as much as a punchline as a plot point, but it was never too far from the characters' consciousness. Everyone knew in those days that New York City was simply not a safe place to be.

Since so many artists of the postmodern era — where visual narrative media like television and film became the primary forms of cultural mass communication — either lived in New York or were from New York, the city was an overwhelmingly common backdrop for the most popular movies and shows. To those outside the city, New York was a place that was almost not a place at all — it was where the imaginary events on the screen in your living room occurred. It had an aura of hyper-reality, a feeling of confusion between what is real and what is simulated. Practically everyone in the world knows New York's major landmarks and street names; we have an incredibly intimate familiarity with it even if we've never been there. The degree of accuracy of our knowledge would probably make a real New Yorker scowl in derision, but the point is that the *sense* of a familiarity is there. To the point where many people who travel to Manhattan for the first time report that it feels more like stepping onto a movie set than being in an actual city. We have a cultural yearning for New York that makes it in some ways inherently nostalgic. The city has become cultural shorthand that carries a great amount of significance.

That New York is just barely a real place that exists on Earth is joked about in the cartoon a lot, as well as in the first movie; when a somewhat-disguised Raphael leaps over the hood of one of NYC's famous yellow taxis while chasing after Casey Jones, we hear a brief conversation between the cab driver and his passenger:

> PASSENGER
> (astonished)
> What the heck was that?

> DRIVER
> (totally nonchalant, and with thick New York accent)
> Looked like kind of a big turtle. In a trench coat. (Pause.)
> You're going to LaGuardia, right?

The other thing that marks New York as the quintessential postmodern location is that it is a pastiche of a city. The legendary first sight new immigrants see upon arriving to the United States is the Statue of Liberty, a symbol of freedom from oppression that is supposed to be America's finest attribute. But at the same time, the very presence of immigrants from all over the world means that New York (and therefore America as a whole) doesn't and can't have one single identity. New York is a hybrid, an experimental combination of those victims of oppression along with others seeking new opportunities, and their descendants.[20] Paradoxically, that quality hasn't made New York the pinnacle of tolerance — certainly not during the late '80s and early '90s when the Turtles were among New York's most famous citizens. Crime in New York was at its peak exactly when Ninja Turtles was at its own (1990), and their influence similarly both began to drop precipitously in 1994, coinciding with the election of Rudy Giuliani. A huge amount of the violent crime was the direct result of racial tensions. In 1989, a black teenager was murdered by a rampaging white mob in one of the most shocking and brutal cases of racial violence in New York's memory. Then in 1991, a Hasidic Jew accidentally struck and killed an African-American child with his car in the Crown Heights neighborhood, and anti-Jewish protests by hundreds of New York's black citizens (including so-called civil rights activist Al Sharpton) quickly descended into a violent riot scarily reminiscent of Kristallnacht, including looting and burning of Jewish-owned homes and businesses, dozens of injuries, and two killings. And in 1993 there was the World Trade Center bombing, a portent of the rising risk to the West from the specter of Islamic terrorism.

TMNT was perfectly positioned to comment on all of this, if only obliquely. As New York was, and is, one of the most racially and culturally diverse cities in the world, and as this is

---

20 Including, it ought to be mentioned, the descendants of people who were kidnapped from West Africa and taken to America to be enslaved (until 1865), segregated (until 1964), and oppressed (your mileage may vary).

at once both a blessing and a curse, the Turtles as non-humans were simultaneously oppressed in the midst of this melting pot and risking their lives to protect it. It *needed* protection from forces both external and internal, and no one could be better suited to the task than the ultimate outsiders, the quintessential hybrids, the Teenage Mutant Ninja Turtles.

Teenageness itself is an utterly postmodern idea. While adolescence is an inherent biological and psychological period of transition and transformation, American entertainment's romanticizing of the 13-to-19-year-old age group as a unique culture unto itself can probably trace its roots only back as far as 1955 and the profoundly influential movie *Rebel Without a Cause*, starring James Dean. The world's moral certainty was badly shaken; "question authority" became a mantra, but outright rejection of any and all authority developed into a full-blown fetish. In the post–World War II world, the generation gap became a kind of Cold War, which *Rebel* strikingly illustrated. The film likely didn't intend to lionize rebellion for its own sake, but instead criticize the perceived rise of juvenile delinquency and the breakdown of effective parenting. Teenageness as a cultural force and state of mind began there and persists to this day; teenagers became ubiquitous in media, including among comic book superheroes like the X-Men in the 1960s. Synonymous with rebellion, teens were the frontline soldiers in the fight against conformity, represented by "the grown-ups." It was a self-imposed Otherness that gained more and more traction as young people saw that the world didn't work the way they felt it ought to.

That the Turtles are teenagers is critical to understanding their position as the ultimate outsiders. Teenageness carries with it a ton of cultural associations — guerrilla warfare against hegemony, the romance of its methods in perfect proportion to the hopelessness of its goals — but more than this, teenageness is marketed as aspirational. Kids who were, say, 10 when they started watching the 16-year-old Turtles on TV could vicariously fight evil, doubtless already feeling cramped by their parents' apparently arbitrary restrictions, and think, *Soon I'll be a teenager too!*

The Turtles cartoon goes further with the teenager trope than the comic did, mostly because it was aimed at a younger audience. That was where the pizza obsession came from — teenagers like pizza, right? — but also the evocations of skateboard and surf culture, most obviously in Michelangelo's trademark catchphrase: *Cowabunga!* The cartoon also pays direct homage to the genesis of the teenager trope in the fourth episode of the first season, "Hot Rodding Teenagers from Dimension X," in which a trio of elfin aliens called the Neutrinos accidentally come to Earth via the Technodrome's dimensional portal. The three Neutrinos are late-1950s-style beatnik-hipsters from outer space, in the mold of Jet Screamer, daughter Judy's rock star crush from *The Jetsons*. They drive rocket-powered lowriders through the sky and execrate their war-torn home dimension as "like, Squaresville, daddy-o!" The Neutrinos are conscientious objectors in a dimension of comprehensive conscription, in which heavy weaponry is required by law even for civilian vehicles. In one particularly overwrought moment, the female Neutrino, Kala, moans, "You don't know what it's like, living in a place where everybody wants to do you in *just for the crime of being young!*" Michelangelo rushes instantly to her side to comfort her, because he's totally trying to get in there. While we might watch that scene and roll our eyes, the thing is *that's how teenagers actually feel*: as if the whole universe is against them. Their values are different, their experiences are different. The Turtles, teenagers themselves, naturally sympathize with the Neutrinos' plight and their rebellion against the polymorphous oppression of their world, and so does the audience — the kids watching at home, within whom the first stirrings of adolescent rebellion have maybe already begun. Yet the Turtles also subvert this trope; in stark contrast to the James Dean archetype, the Turtles can love pizza and skateboarding and horror movies and getting into fights *without* rejecting the moral teachings of their parental figure and the society that he represents. Their rebellion *has* a cause.

Mutantness is obviously the strongest conceptual force throughout the TMNT multiverse. A mutant is something that has been changed from its original or natural form — it's no longer one thing but not yet quite another. Mutation symbolizes Otherness in all kinds of postmodern literature; as mentioned, Kafka and Rushdie have used the trope to great effect. In superhero comics, mutants typically represent the conundrum of newness — the potential and the danger that accompanies progress, gaining freedom from old ideas and prejudices coupled with the threat of losing the stability and meaningful traditions of the past. Marvel Comics' biggest stars are mutants.[21] The Marvel Universe's mutants are often described as being the "next step in human evolution," even given the designation of their own subspecies of humanity, *homo sapiens superior*. In the 1960s, the earliest X-Men comics explained the emergence of mutants as a result of prenatal exposure to atomic radiation, and while later this was retconned into radiation only being the trigger for ancient genetic engineering, the association of mutantness with nuclear decay is significant. The dawn of the Atomic Age and of postmodernity have both been tied to the first use of atomic weapons by the United States against Japan at the close of World War II. Those bombs were the end of the old order and the start of something new, something unprecedented and terrifying. It was the breakdown of what we thought we understood about the world, the first shot across the hull of what would become a baffling war of conflicting identities existing within the same body.

The flood of immigration to Western countries, a new distrust of authority, plus post-catastrophe secularism shattered the solid sense of identity that most people had felt before the war. People started hyphenating their self-descriptions

---

21 Or *mutates* — the difference being that mutants (like the X-Men) are born with their special genetic traits, while mutates (like Spider-Man and the Hulk) are born "normal" but develop powers after a specific incident, usually exposure to radiation. Under the Marvel rubric then, the Turtles would technically be mutates rather than mutants. But I'll keep using the word "mutant" because "Teenage Mutate Ninja Turtles" just doesn't have the same ring to it.

to include their parents' or their own country of origin, their religion or lack thereof, and increasingly their ideological and sexual orientations. The second and third generations down that line, with greater incidence and acceptance of divorce, of interracial marriage,[22] blended families, single-parent families, and other sorts of "post-nuclear" families, were increasingly commonplace; more and more people — maybe even the majority — were no longer capable of (or interested in) fitting themselves into one simple census checkbox.

Around the world there were new and ever-evolving technology, political realities, and kinds of people, and nobody really knew how to deal with these things or what to expect. The mutant was the perfect metaphor: born alongside the detonation of a gamma ray bomb or exposure to a mysterious radioactive substance, transfigured from something common and easily intelligible into something different, bizarre, incomprehensible.

Think about it. Your dad is an orphan, a refugee, arriving in the New World with literally nothing. He loves you unconditionally, but you're not even biologically related to him; you're adopted. You're a crazy mixture of everything that's come before you and everything all around you that you've absorbed growing up. There's never been anyone like you before, but who can understand that? No one but your siblings, because in the whole world, in all of history, they are the only ones who share your unique background and circumstances, all the

---

22 Laws against "miscegenation" were ruled unconstitutional in the United States in 1967, which is pretty late, but a Louisiana judge refused to give a marriage license to an interracial couple *in 2009*.

various strains of cultural DNA battling it out for control of your identity.

You aren't one thing, but you're not quite another. What are you?

You're a mutant.

The other mutant and mutated superheroes, from the mainstream comic publishers, explored similar territory, as we've seen, but there are two major differences in the mutant-ness of, say, the X-Men and that of the Turtles, that allowed the Turtles to eclipse even the Uncanny X-Men in the late 1980s and early 1990s.

First, most of the X-Men, and other superheroes, have invisible, or almost invisible, mutations. When Wolverine's claws are sheathed, he just looks like a short hairy dude. Cyclops is just some guy wearing red sunglasses. Rogue has a white streak in her hair. Big deal. This can make for very good storytelling when your primary metaphor is the marginalization resulting from an unpopular political affiliation, or sexual orientation (as Bobby "Iceman" Drake's parents unironically asked their son in the second X-Men movie, "Have you tried . . . *not* being a mutant?"), which generally do not confer *visible* minority status on a person.[23]

---

23 This subtle but important distinction led to a weird legal dispute — like, in the real world, I mean — where Marvel realized that "dolls" and "toys" were classified differently under U.S. import laws: "toys" are taxed at 6.8% but "dolls" are taxed 12%, and the only difference between a "doll" and a "toy" is that, according to the law, a representation of a human is a doll, and everything else is a toy. X-Men action figures were being classified as dolls, so Marvel had to pay 12% on imports; they realized they could save a lot of money by arguing that, because the X-Men are mutants, they are "non-human creatures," and therefore should be classified as toys instead and taxed at the lower rate. Marvel won. What this ruling means for the mutant rights movement remains to be seen, but presumably Playmates never had this issue with the Turtles toys, because they are clearly and visibly not representations of humans.

With the Turtles, it's immediately apparent that they do not fit into any pre-existing categories. Just like many multi-racial kids, or immigrant kids with foreign accents, or religious kids with unusual styles of dress, the Turtles struggle with sticking out — when they allow themselves to be seen at all, that is.

Some of the X-Men are less than presentable in polite society too, but their identities tend to compensate for that in other ways. Hank McCoy, the Beast, is a big blue fuzzy thing, but he only becomes that way years after enroling in Xavier's school, as a result of a scientific experiment; his original mutation was just that he had really big hands and feet (not kidding). Plus, he has an M.D., and a Ph.D. in mathematics, granting him definite social status. Warren Worthington III, originally known as Angel, then Archangel, then Angel again, has huge feathered wings that are difficult to conceal — but he's also a multimillionaire trust fund kid, which probably makes things easier. The Turtles have no such compensation for their freakish, hybrid visage. Trench coats and cheap, Halloween-costume human masks don't cut it.

The other major difference that sets the Turtles' mutant-ness apart from the X-Men's, and makes them more appealing symbolically and as characters, is their lack of the potential for political influence. X-Men, and mainstream superheroes in general, function primarily as political metaphor; the fight for mutant rights is a big thing in the Marvel Universe. The Turtles though aren't political. They're almost inherently apolitical; they don't actively pursue equal rights with humans, they pretty much just want to live their lives and be left alone. But they can't even venture to the surface without getting called out for being different. X-Men is not so much about identity as it is about *affiliation* — being a mutant in the Marvel Universe locates you as a member of an oppressed subculture, but a subculture whose members, individually and as a group, are explicitly superior to the oppressive majority. TMNT is much more strongly about identity in the literal sense, particularly hybridized identity; the Turtles aren't members of a group of others who are like them, beyond their immediate family — they don't necessarily have any more in common, biologically or culturally, with other mutated animals than they do with humans — and they're pretty much okay with that. For the Turtles, the personal is not political. A hybridized identity, including the alienation and challenges that come along with it, is more or less an inevitable condition of living in the modern world, and coming to terms with that fact — not attempting to overthrow the status quo by violence or persuasion — is what mutant heroism looks like in the world of TMNT.

Ninjaness is yet another factor contributing to the relevance of TMNT to the postmodern generation. On one level, it represents further hybridization of the Turtles' identity: they were born and raised in the United States, they are utterly American, and yet the traditions that their parent taught them are thoroughly Japanese — not even cool, contemporary

Japanese stuff, but an ancient and mysterious tradition[24] that has been basically extinct (or maybe just very, very, very well hidden) for over 200 years. Their Western identity is at odds with their Eastern identity, in terms of values and in terms of the method of assimilation; Japanese tradition was actively instilled in them by Splinter, but their American education came entirely from their passive absorption of pop culture. And it's their Americanness that dominates their personalities and their day-to-day behavior: they prefer pizza to Splinter's sushi, and they don't speak Japanese very well.[25] Leonardo, eldest brother and the Turtles' de facto leader, is closest to Splinter in his identification with their Eastern roots, to the point where Raphael mockingly nicknames him "Splinter Junior." But even Leo prefers a slice and a good sci-fi novel to ramen and anime. This is surely an experience shared by the second- or third-generation Westerners reading and watching the Turtles' exploits, whose own parents or grandparents had attempted to impart a heritage that the kids, craving Westernization, were largely indifferent or even hostile to. Yet this heritage cannot be freely ignored, either. It's just one more piece of the hybrid identity that is, paradoxically, becoming dominant in the postmodern condition.

---

24 Practically a *mythological* tradition, or at a least heavily exoticized one — I'm hesitant to call it Orientalism, which carries pejorative connotations, because in the case of TMNT the ninjaness is more a pastiche of works that could themselves be considered either Orientalist in a negative sense or else just an authentic incorporation of influences that genuinely do come out of Japanese culture.

25 In the third live-action TMNT film, about which more later, when the Turtles are transported to 17th century Japan, Michelangelo attempts to greet one of the locals in his native tongue; he says, "*Ohio, wasabi*," which Raphael translates incredulously and not quite accurately as "Hello, mustard."

The other thing about ninjaness is its requirement of hiddenness. A ninja who can't hide, or who doesn't hide, is no ninja at all. And the Turtles have strong cause to hide from many of the people, and not-exactly-people, in their world. The ninja must be able to move undetected, do whatever needs doing, and then vanish instantly. Of course, this is easier when you're a human being indistinguishable from any other anonymous human being. For a quartet of giant Turtles, if you want to sneak around without being noticed, you're going to have to be pretty effing good at stealth tactics. And if you're, say, the only kid at your school who's a shade more whole wheat than Wonder Bread, or you dress funny or eat weird food, you probably feel that perfecting your disappearing act is of more immediate utility than studying fractions. You learn the best ways not to stick out like a big green thumb. And if it's not possible to literally hide, a bit of *ninjutsu* training would certainly come in handy.

You can see the Turtles acknowledging the tension of their ninjaness in the way they dress. Well, okay, so mostly they go around naked (Turtles are cold-blooded and have retractable, uh, limbs, so there's no sense in them wearing clothes that restrict their movements), but besides the belts where they store their weapons, they all wear *ninja masks*. Why? It's obviously not for the same reason that human ninjas wear masks, i.e., to conceal their identity. Some cloth tied around their big green heads doesn't fool anybody. In the cartoons, the Turtles' masks are different colors, to make it easier to tell them apart,[26] but

---

26 In the 1987 cartoon, the Turtles' belts are also monogrammed, which is just *adorable*.

in the original comic that doesn't work for two reasons: in the Mirage series, the Turtles all wear red masks (which we know from the covers), and anyway the comic is in black-and-white! The real point of the masks seems to be a joke about the paradox of being a ninja turtle, the contradiction between these two seemingly incompatible yet mutually inseparable aspects of their identity. They're ninjas, and ninjas wear masks. The purpose of the mask is rendered void by the creature behind it, and that gap — the disconnect between the mask's intended function and its complete irrelevance when it's a giant turtle wearing it — is the whole point. They rarely take the masks off, further reinforcing that they don't have secret identities — they are always themselves. Superheroes don't wear their costumes when they're just relaxing at home. It's thoroughly postmodern, a little like shirts with the stitching on the outside for no reason, or teenagers swiping their parents' clothes, the fashionability of which derives from how consummately unfashionable they are.

But the Turtles did it first! They've been teenagers since like before you were *born*, son.[27]

Turtleness is the last factor in the TMNT's characterization that signals the hybridity of their identity, and it's also the most visible. They're giant turtles. Half-human and half-animal, but their animal attributes are primarily (though not entirely) the *physical* ones — they're green and have shells — whereas their

---

27 Q: How did the hipster burn his mouth? A: He was eating pizza before it was cool.

human traits are more mental or intellectual — they talk and have human-like psychology, and so on. In part, this sort of hybridity isn't new or tied to postmodernism (mythology and literature has been using the trope of human-like animals for, like, ever), and it symbolizes something that people have been struggling with for the entire history of our self-awareness. But TMNT, again, uses hybridity slightly differently in order to make a statement about the prevailing attitude of postmodernity and why Ninja Turtles rejects it.

You and I and every other person are a combination of a physical animal body and a non-physical human mind.[28] The tension between body and mind is a major theme in everything in which humans have ever engaged — art, religion, philosophy, everything. The physical body wants physical stuff, like food and sex and punching things, and the non-physical mind wants non-physical stuff, like beauty and morality. Finding the balance between these often conflicting impulses is what characterizes much of what we're doing when we're trying to understand how a person should be. But animals don't do this. Animals, according to this system, are all body and no mind. They behave, but their behavior is solely a series of reactions to physical stimuli, not the result of intellectual reflection. They may have psychology (or, if you like, personality, a characteristic pattern of behavior related to sensory input

---

28 Please don't get on me about describing the mind as non-physical, okay? If you're one of those materialist zealots and it makes you feel better, you can call it a metaphor, but the *mind* as distinct from the *brain* is not a physical, observable-by-the-senses kind of thing. I'm going to defer to philosopher David Chalmers, author of *The Conscious Mind*, who very convincingly argues that "consciousness cannot logically supervene on the physical." Go bug him.

and learned responses), but they don't have *phenomenology* (or qualia, i.e., the subjective character of experience, conscious self-awareness, that *what-it's-like*ness that gives sense data its literal and figurative flavor). Whatever animals do, it's motivated purely by instinct and physical impulses — and I include emotions in that category. Humans are the only creatures we know of that are capable of acting out of principle, that can do a thing or not do it *purely because it's right or wrong*.

Because the Turtles look more like turtles than like humans, most people who encounter them at first think of them as monsters. It's only when the Turtles show that they *think* like humans, not like animals, that people are able to relate to them as they would to another human. The reason that the Turtles and other mutants of their ilk are outcasts from society is not ideological — they're not shunned because of the way they think or the way they behave — it is pure prejudice based on the way that they look.

This in itself is a pretty old story, but what TMNT does is approach it in a refreshingly retrogressive direction; from the postmodernist's point of view, what Turtles does is so conservative that it's practically counterrevolutionary. In the best possible way, if you ask me.

As we've seen, the other aspects of TMNT hook very deliberately to postmodern ideas and arguments. So you'd think that on the animal/human hybridity issue, it would do the same thing: that is, deconstruct and undermine or problematize traditional morality. But what it actually does is almost the exact opposite. What makes the Turtles not monsters isn't just that they can talk, or that they eat pizza and watch television. It's the fact that they adhere scrupulously to a received moral code. There are other mutant turtles in the TMNT universe — there's Slash, and there's Tokka from the second live-action film — but they are bad guys, they're monsters. Not because they can't talk or don't like pizza, but because they don't follow any system of ethics.

As a matter of fact, the Turtles' morality is what presents the contradiction with *all* the other aspects of their identity. Teenagers, mutants, and ninjas are all known for their opposition to conventional systems. Animals too have no behavioral restrictions besides those mandated by nature. But the Teenage Mutant Ninja Turtles have a deep-seated respect for authority when it is earned, and a fundamental piece of their self-image is bound up with following an ancient and objective code of conduct that dictates how they are meant to behave in order to be good. In other words, they cleave unapologetically to a Grand Narrative — which basically equates to a ferocious ninja kick to postmodernism's big stupid face.

Jean-François Lyotard diagnosed the era-that-came-after-modernism in his book *The Postmodern Condition*; it was first published in French in 1979, when Frank Miller was initiating the postmodernization of superhero comics, and translated into English in 1984, contemporaneous with the publication of *TMNT* #1. Lyotard writes that the postmodern condition is, at its core, an "incredulity towards metanarratives." Meaning that the citizens of postmodernity, because of historical horrors like the Holocaust, and the ubiquity of science and technology like television and atomic bombs, have lost their faith in the kind of Big Stories that gave meaning to life in past eras. This includes religion, political ideologies, and even the sense of historical progress that gave us reason to think the future would be an improvement on the past. Lyotard didn't himself actually assert that nothing was real (although thinkers following him kind of tended to ignore that bit), but he did say that since history and science have made us now incontrovertibly aware that we can't possibly ever know for sure what is real, Grand Narratives have given way to local narratives, smaller stories that behave more democratically. Whereas in the past it was assumed that the Truth would eventually win out, when all hope of truth is gone, what we get instead is that the most popular stories gain all the perquisites of fact regardless of their actual relationship to reality. It's closely related to the concept of *truthiness* popularized by Stephen Colbert. It's the preference for subjectivity over objectivity; the phenomenon of authority deriving not from resemblance to what is the case in the world, but from who has the strongest convictions. It's the placebo effect writ large. Clap your hands if you believe in fairies.

Ninja Turtles averts this *so hard*.

Everything about the Turtles establishes them as the most postmodern of all. The world they live in is a hyperreal, exaggeratedly mutated version of our own, where the melting pot of conflicting narratives created by globalized communication and transmigration swells to include: mutant animals, space aliens, telepathy and mind-transfers, ghosts, cyborgs, demons, time travel, parallel universes, magic pencils, dudes made out of rocks . . . pretty much everything but the kitchen sink. This is exactly the kind of thing that Lyotard says invariably leads to the dissolution of our confidence in Grand Narratives. But the Turtles aren't shaken for a second. Their position in postmodernity allows them to fight evil ninjas in New York City in one issue, then be taken thousands of years into the past by a Valley Girl with a techno-magical golden scepter from the 79th Level of Null-Time, whatever that is, in the next. You'd think that all these opposing, if not outright contradictory, narratives would undermine the Turtles' confidence in the principles they were raised to believe in. That's certainly what Lyotard insists that postmodernism does to people. But no. Their adherence to the Truth is not degraded.

Despite having every reason to be, the Turtles are not incredulous toward metanarratives. And this is a pretty big deal. I'm not saying that Eastman and Laird had read Lyotard,[29] but their work is a powerful refutation of the epistemology (theory of knowledge) that Lyotard sets out in *The Postmodern Condition*. Readers and viewers of TMNT strongly respond to this, whether consciously or not, because despite the insanity of postmodern existence and the exhausting strain of living with a hybrid identity (and the Turtles' identity is as hybrid as its gets), they haven't resigned themselves to the futility of metanarratives either. TMNT proves — not singularly, but most clearly and most entertainingly — that personal and rational confidence in an objective moral system

---

29 Though they might have, I don't actually know.

can survive even the most ridiculous gobbledygook that the universe throws at you.[30] This, in a way, has TMNT prefiguring the anti-ironic trend in art and literature that's come to be called "Remodernism" or "The New Sincerity," most visibly championed by people like the multimedia artist Billy Childish and author David Foster Wallace (peace be upon him).[31] So despite the fact that everything about the Turtles is postmodern to the core, they ultimately reject the relativism, hopelessness, and arbitrary anti-authoritarianism that by all accounts they ought to embrace. It's their fierce opposition to the cynical ideology of their time, the adherence to an "uncool" moral framework that mostly doesn't even benefit them, that makes us want them to succeed all the more.

---

30 To be fair, Lyotard later admitted that when he wrote *The Postmodern Condition* he didn't know what he was talking about, in some places misunderstood and in others deliberately mischaracterized the works he cited in support of his hypothesis, and in fact referred to that book as his worst, and as — oh man, get this — *a parody*. I think he just meant "parody" in the pejorative sense, as in the book was stupid, not that he was intentionally trying to satirize anything, but his use of that word is extremely telling given all the pomo connotations of pastiche that we've already talked about. Lyotard's palinode came after people had started to realize that incredulity toward metanarratives is itself a kind of metanarrative, so what even the hell.

31 Which, I know what you're thinking, but DFW didn't, like, *invent* footnotes, okay?

3

The Rise and Fall of Turtle Power

Turtlemania hit full stride between 1989 and 1991. Mirage was publishing a second title called *Tales of the Teenage Mutant Ninja Turtles*, with stories that jumped around throughout Turtles continuity. Stories took place between the issues of the original, still ongoing comic (which was appropriate since there were many issues of the original series telling stories outside of continuity during this period). Debuting on December 14, 1987, the cartoon had launched its own new continuity — a very toned-down one, but the main wellspring of the Turtles' popularity — which spawned yet another comic book series, published by Archie Comics, called *Teenage Mutant Ninja Turtles Adventures*. It was printed in full-color (the Mirage books were still black and white) and started out with a three-issue miniseries that adapted the first season of the cartoon, then four issues that continued directly adapting the TV show; after that, it began telling original stories and would eventually veer way off from the plot, feel, and tone of its parent series. It would grow weirder and darker than the cartoon, and skew heavily toward environmental issues and even world politics. *Adventures*, the first "third-generation" spawn of *TMNT*, represents the first sub-sub-universe for the Turtles, the first adaptation of an adaptation, a comic based on a cartoon based on a comic. It serves as the major example of another of TMNT's greatest strengths when it comes to mining the postmodern zeitgeist for relevance as well as sheer longevity: *multiple histories*.

One consequence of the dissolution of Grand Narratives in the postmodern era was that suddenly no one could agree on what history was, or at least on what kind of history we should be teaching. Was Christopher Columbus a great and heroic explorer or the harbinger of an unprecedented genocide? Which side actually won the War of 1812? Was the American Civil War a War Between the States or a War of Northern Aggression? Was the entire universe created by God less than 6,000 years ago, or was it the result of blind cosmic forces over a period of billions of years? None of these questions were new to postmodernism, but now that distrust of Grand Narratives was a pervasive part of society, opposing whatever the authorities professed became an automatically political act. Holding unpopular beliefs became a badge of pride. Your position on Kirk v. Picard was as definitional an issue as your position on *Roe v. Wade*.

This might not sound like it has very much to do with Ninja Turtles, but it does, in the sense that art and entertainment reacted to the rising skepticism by offering multiple versions of the same thing targeted at different groups, different demographics, whose receptivity to a work would vary. Again, I'm not trying to argue that Bowdlerization was anything original to postmodernism — editor Thomas Bowdler expurgated the violent, profane, and sexy bits from Shakespeare two-and-a-half centuries ago — but whereas censorship of works to make them more appropriate for certain audiences (usually children) had been going on forever, the multiple versions of TMNT were created not for moral reasons but for artistic and commercial ones. It was also possible to access all these different versions of the same thing simultaneously: you could read the original comic, watch the cartoon, then read the comic based on the cartoon. It's all TMNT, but everything that happens is totally different in each and every one of them. You could keep reading the original comic and pretend that the cartoon doesn't exist, because it's for kids and you like your entertainment more grown-up. Or you could, like I did, discover the cartoon as a child and be instantly entranced, then find the comic based on the cartoon and be bewildered but no less entranced, and only later read the original comics that will become your new favorite, definitive version of the Turtles — but only because, had you stumbled upon that original version when it had first appeared, before you ever the saw the cartoon (when you were, uh, five), you would have had no idea what was going on, no context to understand it, and no stomach for the kind of brutality that occurred in its pages, let alone the capacity to appreciate the layers upon layers of references contained therein.

This multiplicity, the divergence of a single work of art into a spray of contradictory worlds where you can select the one that appeals to you the most and have that be the *real* one, continued to proliferate. TMNT became a true transmedia franchise. There were video games: based loosely on the cartoon (so, again, another adaptation of an adaptation), the first TMNT game came out in 1989 for the original 8-bit Nintendo Entertainment System. An action game with both overhead and side-scrolling aspects (a bit similar, although far superior, to the fairly disappointing *Zelda 2: The Adventure of Link*), it was, as Nintendo games tended to be in those days, unaccountably hard. If you didn't have an NES at home, there was also the arcade game, again based on the cartoon, but a side-scrolling beat-em-up in the tradition of *Double Dragon*. It featured a simultaneous four-player mode, fantastic (for the time) graphics and sound, and a healthy dash of humor. The arcade game was ported to consoles in 1990 as a sequel to the original NES game, even though there was absolutely no connection between the two, and the end of the NES game actually contradicted what occurred in the arcade game. Then an actual sequel to the arcade game came out in 1991: *Turtles in Time*, where the Turtles, uh, traveled through time. It was the bestselling arcade game ever. It was also ported to consoles (*TMNT 4: Turtles in Time*, after the third game, *TMNT 3: The Manhattan Project*, another original NES game, came out in 1992). When the big hot thing was fighting games (thanks to the success of *Street Fighter 2*), there was *TMNT: Tournament Fighters* (1993), a game that pitted players against each other as any of the Turtles, characters from the cartoon, the original comics, and the Archie comics series, or original characters — a synthesis of disparate TMNT continuities that drew fans of any and every version of the franchise, and stood as a testament to the extreme flexibility of TMNT. It should also be noted that the archetypes of the four Turtles were very consistently and effectively used throughout all of the TMNT games, a major factor in their success. Even with the limited interactivity of games at that time, the Turtles' individual personalities shone through in their movements and fighting styles.[32] Maintaining the thematic heart of what made TMNT so popular while at the same time allowing for profound flex-ibility across every imaginable medium made it possible for the Turtles to dominate the increasingly Turtle-saturated cul-ture of the 1990s.

Synthesis is what characterized later incarnations of the Turtles. Once there were multiple continuities from which to draw, each originating from a common source but then veering off on its own, new works that emerged had increas-ingly more material to incorporate that would be at once new and familiar. The Archie comics did some of this, and the video games did a bit more, but what really took full advan-tage of the storytelling possibilities of nesting references and

---

32 In every single one of these games, Donatello was the best Turtle to use. He was the slowest moving, but he had the longest reach and hit the hardest; q.v. the first TMNT game for NES, which, as far as I can tell, *could not be beaten without using Donatello on the final level.* Just more evidence, as if you needed it, to prove that Donnie is Best Turtle.

combining elements from numerous incarnations were the Teenage Mutant Ninja Turtles movies.

The big deal about the first TMNT film was that it would be live-action, with actors in animatronic suits portraying the Turtles. Animatronics, first invented in the 1960s by the Walt Disney Company, is itself a hybrid art form, combining special-effects modeling and puppetcraft, mechanical engineering and robotics, and, in the case of humanoid characters, acting. At the time that the original Turtles movies were produced, animatronics was far more advanced than computer-generated special effects; as we all know, effects are probably the number-one factor that makes or breaks an audience's ability to suspend its disbelief as alien or fantastical creatures interact with human actors onscreen. In a live-action film, puppets or costumes that looked fake or unconvincing would be fatal, since a huge part of TMNT's thematic appeal is playing these unlikely characters totally straight.[33] It was 1990, the very highest height of the Turtles' popularity, but a bad first movie could have crashed things pretty severely.

It portended well for the film that the costumes were done by Jim Henson's company, which was at the forefront of non-computer-generated special effects technology. It's entirely due to the Jim Henson Company's expertise that the movie doesn't look nearly as dated today as it could — the costumes seem primitive, but not nearly as much as the third movie's,

---

[33] We should all thank God that Eastman and Laird turned down the first offer they got for a film adaptation of their comic; notorious B-movie director Roger Corman proposed a movie with the Turtles played by comedians in green makeup.

which ditched the Henson Company's top-quality and very expensive animatronics.[34] The movie was produced by New Line Cinema, the indie production company responsible for the early Nightmare on Elm Street films. Rather than going with a major studio (which Eastman and Laird easily could have done, given the already monumental success of the franchise), they went with an independent, staying true to the non-corporate roots of the franchise, and it shows — in a good way. It was a high-stakes movie, but with a relatively small company at the helm, there was minimal executive interference. That attitude carried into the film's plot as well, and a Turtles movie that cost only $13 million ended up making $200 million at the box office, making it one of that year's top ten highest-earning films. TMNT became the model case of an indie comic becoming a ridiculously huge success.

As far as I can tell, the only two indie-comics movies that were produced before the first Turtles film and could be considered successes were 1972's *Tales from the Crypt* movie, adapted from the EC Comics series by British horror production company Amicus Productions, and 1981's *Heavy Metal*, the animated and very not-for-kids adaptation of the often pornographic science-fiction-and-fantasy comics magazine of the same name (which starred most of the cast of SCTV for some reason). *Heavy Metal* was a huge influence on Kevin Eastman; he went on to buy the magazine with some of his Turtles money. *Tales from the Crypt* and *Heavy Metal* are very different from the

---

34 The second TMNT movie is dedicated to the memory of Henson, who passed away during its production.

kind of indie-comics movies that were made after 1990's *Teenage Mutant Ninja Turtles*. Both were anthology films (rather than having a single overriding storyline), and neither was in any way toned down to reach wider or younger audiences. There had, of course, been many mainstream comic-book movies that had been successes, but they were mostly big-budget all-ages super-hero things. Once *Teenage Mutant Ninja Turtles* came along and showed that you could be true to the independent spirit of the source material in terms of storytelling and production while also courting mainstream audiences, studios started to learn how to do it right, resulting in artistically successful adaptations like *The Crow* (1994), *Ghost World* (2001), *Hellboy* (2004), *Scott Pilgrim vs. the World* (2010), and so on.

The reviews were mediocre. Roger Ebert, damning with faint praise, wrote in the *Chicago Sun-Times*: "This movie is nowhere near as bad as it might have been, and probably is the best possible Teenage Mutant Ninja Turtle movie." Another review, from the *New York Times* no less, which insists on repeatedly misspelling the title with a superfluous hyphen (*Teen-Age Mutant Ninja Turtles*, which is a lot like Mr. Burns remarking on how much he's enjoying "this so-called *iced cream*,") points out, not complimentarily, that "the film, while silly, is considerably less cute than the television show, and in fact isn't really geared to young viewers. It is itself a mutant of sorts, a contentious, unsightly hybrid of martial-arts exploitation film and live-action cartoon."

But what could you expect? The real triumph of the first Turtles movie is the incredibly successful merging of storylines from the original comic with the elements from the cartoon that its younger viewers would expect when they entered the theater. The plotline is essentially torn straight from issues #1, #2, and #10 of the Mirage comic, but April O'Neil is a reporter, like in the cartoon, and the cartoon Turtles' obsessive love of pizza and silly surf-inspired catchphrases also make the transition to live-action.[35] The film wasn't nearly as violent as the comic, but significantly more so than the cartoon; the inclusion of Casey Jones, hockey-mask-wearing, borderline-sociopathic vigilante, assured that. In the cartoon, Casey only appears a handful of times; in the comic, he is one of the Turtles' most trusted allies. Putting Casey in the movie had the potential to alienate kids (while giving April O'Neil a love interest, which also, to be fair, could have alienated kids), but he was such a fundamental part of the original comic that to leave him out entirely would have presented problems. They kept him, and the movie is all the better for it. At the end of the movie, when Shredder is thrown off the roof of a building by Splinter and lands in a parked garbage truck, Casey *straight up murders him*, pulling the truck's trash-compactor switch with a gleeful "oops!" and we watch Shredder's helmet get crushed flat. For a movie aimed primarily at kids, that was a ballsy move. Kudos to you, New Line.

That first movie showed exactly how good a Turtles product could be by taking advantage of TMNT's own

---

35 We also had the thrill of swearing, with Raphael screaming "DAMN!" multiple times. Very true to the original comic; pretty shocking for a kid who was only familiar with the cartoon.

greatest strength: its mutability. In creating a pastiche of a pastiche, they did new things with TMNT without alienating the invested audience, because they stayed true to its core themes and tropes. At the same time, entirely original characters and ideas were created as well — for future incarnations to mine for thematic resonance *and* nostalgic value.[36]

The following year, *Teenage Mutant Ninja Turtles II: The Secret of the Ooze* did the same thing, although somewhat less successfully. It cost $25 million to make and took in close to $79 million at the box office — much less profitable than its predecessor, but still the 13th-highest grossing film of 1991. Again, the reviews were mixed at best. Donna Britt of the *Washington Post* teamed up with her son, Hamani Britt-Gibson, to write an overall condescending review wherein the kid insisted it was better than the original, and the mom says she preferred the first one because it "was more mystical — darker, with more allusions to Eastern religion. It spent more time encouraging kids to be patient, and to find strength within themselves. Director Michael Pressman made the sequel brighter, sunnier — much more like a traditional kids cartoon. . . . The second TMNT has enough jokes aimed at adults to make for a relatively painless outing for parents forced to take their kids to see it."

Roger Ebert disliked the movie enough that he didn't even really bother to actually review it, but what he did write is

---

36 Jumping ahead a little bit, in my opinion the writer who's best at doing this — synthesizing the very best from every TMNT incarnation and making it thrive in its new context — is Tristan Jones. He worked on *Volume 4* of Mirage's TMNT book and *Volume 2* of *Tales of the TMNT*, and he managed to rescue characters from the movies and cartoons and transport them into Mirage's original continuity; when you think about how serious the original continuity is compared to its younger-skewing spawn, this is a pretty major achievement.

fascinating in itself, for both the insights and the misreadings of who the Turtles are and what they're all about, so it's worth quoting here at length:

> Kids like the turtles. A recent national survey reported that 95 percent of grade school teachers could trace aggressive, antisocial classroom behavior to the Ninja Turtles — high praise. As someone who was raised on Superman, Batman, Spiderman [sic], and Wonder Woman, I think the kids are getting the short end of the stick. What kind of a superhero is a reptile who lives in sewers, is led by a rat, eats cold pizza, and is the product of radioactive waste? Is this some kind of a cosmic joke on the kids, robbing them of their birth-right, a sense of wonder? Or is it simply an emblem of our drab and dreary times? One disturbing thing about the turtles is that they look essentially the same. All that differentiates them, in the Nintendo game that gave them birth, is their weapons. It's as if the whole sum of a character's personality is expressed by the way he does violence. The turtles are an example of the hazards of individuality.
>
> They hang out together, act together, fight together, and have a dim collective IQ that expresses itself in phrases like "Cowabunga, dude." This is the way insecure teenage boys sometimes talk in a group, as a way of creating solidarity, masking fears of inad-equacy, and forming a collective personality that is

stupider than any individual member of it. The way you attain status in the group is by using violence to defend it against outsiders. People raised on these principles run a risk of starring in videotapes of police brutality.

I liked the older superheroes better. The ones that stood out from a crowd, had their own opinions, were not afraid of ridicule, and symbolized a future of truth and justice. Spiderman [sic] and Superman represented democratic values. Today's kids are learning from the Turtles that the world is a sinkhole of radioactive waste, that it's more reassuring to huddle together in sewers than take your chances competing at street level, and that individuality is dangerous. Cowabunga.

Besides the fact that Ebert seems to have thought that the Turtles video game predated the comic, his biases are incredibly intriguing. He didn't like the Turtles because he liked Superman. He couldn't relate to the Turtles' brotherhood, to their outsiderness, to their youth. While correctly identifying that the Turtles' popularity is a reflection of the age in which we live, he disdained their origins, made fun of their parentage and their home, and dismissed them as being identical despite their very distinctive personalities — if their skin was, say, brown instead of green, he'd never have gotten away with talking about them like that. What's more, he believed that Superman represents individuality. Basically, he was an old white guy who had no idea what it's like to be a member of an oppressed group, and no memory of what it was like to be young and idealistic.

People hate on *Turtles II* because they remember it as the Turtles movie that had Vanilla Ice in it — which it was — but where it succeeds, it succeeds very strongly. The plot skewed closer to the cartoon than to the comic, which was maybe its first mistake, but it also took chances by not giving the cartoon's audience exactly what they thought they'd wanted. The plot threads from the original Mirage comic are still pretty strong here: the Turtles need to find a new home after their lair had been found and destroyed by the Foot in the first movie; and they also fall into a quest for their origins — the "secret of the ooze" referred to in the title — which leads them to the mysterious corporation known in this universe as Techno-Global Research Industries (changed from Techno-Cosmic Research Industries in the original comic) and the discovery that the ooze that had led to their creation was nothing but a waste by-product. An accident. When the Turtles find out about this, it leads to what I always thought was a genuinely touching moment; Donatello has a bit of an existential crisis realizing that their creation was nothing but "a big mistake," lamenting: "I thought there'd be something . . . I thought we'd find out we were *special*."

Splinter, the ever-supportive father, consoles Donnie with some very sensible wisdom, saying, "Do not confuse the specter of your origin with your present worth, my son." The Turtles came from nothing and yet they've grown up to contribute real value in the world; that's a message that many kids, growing up seeing themselves perhaps as unwanted, often as literal refugees, could definitely latch onto.

Everyone, at the time, had assumed that the second

TMNT movie would include popular villains from the cartoon, such as Krang, and Shredder's mutant henchmen Bebop and Rocksteady. Maybe, the rumors ran, we'd even get to see the Technodrome! But that didn't happen. When Shredder returns, having somehow survived, and learns that some of the mutagen still exists, he kidnaps a scientist from TGRI, Professor Jordan Perry, and forces him to create two new mutants — a snapping turtle, Tokka, and a wolf, Rahzar — that he hopes to use to destroy the Turtles. Professor Perry complies but clandestinely contaminates the ooze so that the resulting mutants have diminished intellectual capacity. Were new characters created to sell new toys? Sure. But at the same time, the story unfolded in a way that was true to the overarching message of TMNT: Tokka and Rahzar were enemies, but they weren't inherently evil or even malicious — they were the result of events outside their understanding, not to mention bad parenting — carrying on the theme that modern identity is complex and hybridized, and a result of forces totally beyond our control.

The humor is also really sharp. One of the funniest lines from any Turtles story comes from this movie: when Leo, Don, and Mike are sneaking in to the Foot Clan's makeshift junkyard hideout to rescue a captured Raphael, the following exchange occurs:

(The three Turtles approach the junkyard's entrance.)

DONATELLO
The perimeter's quiet . . .

LEONARDO
Yeah, a little too quiet.

(There are only two Foot soldiers on guard duty, and the Turtles dispense with them effortlessly.)

DONATELLO
Well, that was easy.

LEONARDO
Yeah, a little too easy.

(They move deeper into the junkyard and see Raphael gagged and bound to a wooden pole.)

DONATELLO
Look! It's Raph!

MICHELANGELO
Yeah, a little too Raph.

That cracks me up every single time — I was even laughing as I typed it out just now — while also perfectly encapsulating the Turtles' personalities and the character of their brotherly relationship.

And yes, Vanilla Ice is in the movie, and that was a misstep. A kind of cynical appeal to the lowest-common-denominator for the sake of commerce at the expense of authenticity, it was a stunt to capitalize on the popularity of a contemporary entertainer who had the fastest-selling hip hop album of all time[37] on the chance that Vanilla Ice fans who weren't necessarily Turtles fans would buy a movie ticket and inflate the box office gross. Rather than using him as an ironic reference or a reverent homage, he was used purely because he was what was popular at that moment — and this is a mistake that we'll see reoccur later, in the couple of TMNT outings that were so disastrous that even the creators have disavowed them, during what I call "The Dark Times."

But think about it this way: first of all, it could have been much worse — Vanilla Ice's appearance in the movie isn't much more than a cameo, he's never referred to by name and has no plot significance; he just happens to be performing at a club into which the fighting spills during the movie's climax. And second: "Ninja Rap" is by far Vanilla Ice's best song ever, and you might as well just admit it.

The third movie, coming out two years later in 1993, was another step down from what the first had accomplished. In some ways it was an admirable attempt to move closer to the Mirage end of the synthesis, after *Secret of the Ooze* had come dangerously close to the cartoon side of things (ignoring that the similarity in tone made the original movie an important bridge between cartoon and comic, and between parent and child). But in other ways, *Turtles III* was difficult to take seriously. The basic plot was taken from the comics, sort of, in

---

37 *Sigh.*

that the Turtles are transported back in time to ancient Japan by a magical golden scepter. But while the arc that occurred in the Mirage comics a year or so earlier was actually one of the best stories ever told in the original timeline, *TMNT III* is the worst of the films. It was profitable, making over $42 million with a $21 million budget, but was reviewed even more poorly than the previous two. *Time Out* rather fairly states that "The first *Teenage Mutant Ninja Turtles* was, for all its faults, a minor miracle. Here, for small children, were heroes who were streetwise, anti-authority, and loved to fight. It couldn't last. In their third film, which is shorn of nearly all the elements which made the Ninjas popular, Raphael pontificates: 'Fighting's for grown-ups, and only if they've got no other choice.' The real Raphael would never say that. One of the most enjoyable things about the Turtles was their interaction with a modern city. Here, however, writer/director Gillard misguidedly sends them back to medieval Japan. The wisecracks have been cut back, and where once the Ninjas' dude-speak was original (influencing, for example, *Wayne's World*) it's now merely imitative."[38]

Though certainly disappointing, it's remembered as worse than it actually was, and it really does have more than a few redeeming qualities. It suffered from sporadically lame writing

---

[38] *Time Out* wasn't wrong about the Turtles' influence on *Wayne's World*, by the way; as originally conceived in the late '80s, Wayne and Garth were supposed to be high school students, and their mode of speech was in tune with the surfer and skater subculture slang that the Turtles introduced to young audiences. By the time those kids were old enough to stay up late and watch *Saturday Night Live*, they already had a familiarity with the argot used in "Wayne's World," even if they didn't yet understand all the references to 1970s heavy metal bands. This certainly contributed to the popularity of the Wayne's World movies among that age group, who really should have been too young to appreciate them.

and inferior animatronics — the Turtles' lip-synchronization is distractingly bad, and Splinter looks particularly robotic. Comparing it to the rest of the Turtles stuff going on at the same time — the Mirage and Archie comics, the cartoon, as well as its live-action film predecessors which were still in very recent memory — it couldn't help but come out as a loser. The comic on which it was loosely based fed on the series' rich history, tied up loose ends, introduced a fierce new villain (the mysterious dinosaur samurai Chote — pronounced *cho*-tay, I think) and gave us new insight into the Turtles' place in the world and the origins of the Foot Clan. The movie, on the other hand, gave us a plot that felt arbitrary, a villain less threatening than any we'd seen before, and an entire village that was astonishingly accepting of a quartet of random *kappa* (demons) showing up to save the day. The four samurai warriors who were transported to 20th century New York in the B-plot, with Casey Jones as their babysitter, fared much worse than the Turtles did in 17th century rural Japan. It's not that it wasn't as *believable* as the last two movies; it just seemed trivial and charmless.

TMNT was peaking in its popularity; it was 1993, and as the franchise expanded more and more, Kevin Eastman and Peter Laird spent more and more time administering the business end of things. Their personal and professional relationship suffered. Following the excellent "Return to New York" storyline in the spring of 1989 (where the Turtles finally come out of hiding and decide to locate and eliminate the resurrected Shredder for the last time), the comic was farmed out to other indie creators for the next four years, becoming more of an anthology series than an ongoing narrative, with out-of-continuity stories and many writers/artists who'd never worked on the Turtles before. This period was extremely hit or miss, with some of the best *TMNT* stories ever being published (Rick Veitch's "Down to the River" and "Soul's Winter" by Stephen Murphy and Michael Zulli are conspicuous highlights), right along with some of the very worst (the issues by Mark Martin and by Rich Hedden and Tom McWeeney are the most egregious).

Episodes of the cartoon during this period were of similarly sporadic quality. Since the show was targeted at kids, it had to conform to the standards of the time, which limited the amount of violence to which the country's precious youth were exposed. Rather than following in the footsteps of martial arts movies and action comics, many of the cartoon episodes took their inspiration, appropriately enough, from classic and contemporary science fiction movies — to name a few: *The Incredible Shrinking Man*, *The Fly*, *Alien*, *RoboCop*, *Attack of the 50 Foot Woman*, *Tarzan at the Earth's Core*, *Invasion of the Body Snatchers*, *Flash Gordon Conquers the Universe*, *Frankenstein*, *The Day the Earth Stood Still*, *Beginning of the End*, and Ed Wood's greatest triumph, *Plan 9 from Outer Space*.

Despite the constraints of Saturday morning, the best episodes of the cartoon nevertheless maintained the themes and overall message that had run through TMNT from the beginning and made it so relevant and relatable. There's honestly so much to say about every single episode of the series that if

I did, this book would end up longer than *Bleak House*. But I will highlight a few examples from its ratings heyday, just to give you a sense of the genuine depth that you may or may not have picked up on if you were watching the show during its original run.

One early stand-out was the episode in which Baxter Stockman is transformed into a mutant fly. An obvious homage to the 1958 movie *The Fly* (and to a lesser extent the remake by David Cronenberg released only a couple of years before this episode), "Enter: The Fly" is notable for its darker elements. For most of the episode, April O'Neil lies near death after being poisoned by the Shredder (as opposed to just a couple of episodes earlier, when he did nothing worse than tie her to a chair), and Baxter's mutation itself is harrowing in its ruthlessness. Krang throws Baxter into a disintegrator chamber to be annihilated, not for any particular crime but just because he doesn't need the help of any pathetic earthling. Baxter survives by having his DNA combined in the disintegrator with a fly that happened to have been following him, but the fact that Krang had so carelessly ordered Baxter's execution is fairly chilling for a kids show of the time.

Baxter is, in a way, the most sympathetic character of this episode: Shredder blames him for a defeat that was not Baxter's fault, then Krang attempts to incinerate him like so much trash, and he ends up mutated against his will. Sadly, Baxter's mind is affected by the transformation; when he escapes and seeks out Shredder to exact revenge, Shredder convinces him that it was the Turtles who were responsible. The Turtles are actually kind of dicks to Baxter, who doesn't really deserve it, and you end up feeling profoundly sorry for this formerly brilliant scientist whose whole life has been ruined by getting tangled up with the megalomaniacal Shredder. Baxter's perpetual victimhood, as well as his fundamental loneliness resulting from his involuntary physical transformation, became a running theme in the other episodes he appeared in (he tended to pop up once a season or so).

Another episode had the Turtles noticing Splinter falling into a depression and, realizing that he missed being human (remember that in the cartoon, Splinter was the mutated version of Hamato Yoshi), Donatello uses the small amount of mutagen left over from their creation to create an antidote and return Splinter to his original human form. Splinter's response to the Turtles' plan is touching: "To be human once more; to walk the streets, to feel the sunlight. How often have I dreamed of this." But what's maybe even more heart-wrenching is Michelangelo's reaction to his sensei's sentiments; he begins to cry and says, "Yeah, I know the feeling." When the antimutagen works, and Splinter returns to being human, he decides to go up to the surface and take his first casual walk in 15 years. The Turtles encourage him to go, but as soon as he leaves, they're in full teen angst mode. Now that Splinter is human again and can live above ground among his own kind, the Turtles aren't sure he's going to come back. They wonder about this aloud, and for the rest of the episode, this specter hangs over them. That's how alienated they are: there's a part of them that can't shake the feeling that their father only stays with them because he has no choice. This storyline surely resonated with kids going through instability in their own families; this was the late '80s, remember, and it's guaranteed that many of the viewers' parents were going through divorces and other kinds of turmoil sure to shake up anyone's self-confidence and identity. The Turtles' insecurity relates back to the overarching theme of defining family that runs through the franchise (and is also extremely prevalent in the first live-action film).

While the main plot is a Lovecraftian tale where the Turtles learn that Shredder has concocted a plan to gain access to Dimension X without Krang's help (using an ancient spellbook he found at the public library — their interlibrary loan system must be super impressive), Splinter realizes that his nostalgia for humanity was misplaced: people are rude and hostile toward him for his unusual mode of dress and the fact that he hasn't got any money. Worse is when the antimutagen starts to wear off; as Splinter begins transforming back into a rat, he ends up being chased down by a frantic mob of people and, eventually, the police. He escapes back to the sewers — barely — and assists the Turtles in preventing Shredder from opening a portal to Dimension X.

When the Turtles say how sorry they are that Splinter's humanity wasn't permanent (though they have to be at least a little bit relieved), Splinter expresses a kind of shocking sentiment: "Seeing how humans treat one another," he says, "I prefer to be an animal." Sour grapes? Maybe. But look, the moral of this story — at a time when children's programs were required by law to have some educational content — was that *people suck*. The overarching theme of TMNT that problematizes the conceptual parallels between human/animal, morality/amorality, and normality/monstrousness through the paradoxical hybridization of mutantness is particularly apparent here.

Also notable was an episode where the host of a national tabloid talk show (clearly modeled after Morton Downey Jr., who at the time had a controversial program that became the model for the sideshow styling and deliberate provocation in shows hosted by Jerry Springer and even Rush Limbaugh and Glenn Beck) was getting huge ratings by going on the air and slandering the Turtles, now well known. Despite their best efforts to remain hidden, their enemies had no such interest, and they often ended up fighting in public. The host derides the Turtles as a menace to society and wonders why the authorities aren't doing more to hunt them down. To try to clear their name, the Turtles appear on the show (remotely, from the basement of the TV station, rather than in front of the usual live studio audience). Stricken with stage fright, they defend themselves very poorly against the host's venomous accusations, but when Krang attacks the TV station with a stolen military vehicle that's a lot like ED-209 from *RoboCop*, the Turtles prove themselves to be heroes by defeating him. The host thanks the Turtles for saving his life, and yet cheerfully admits that he's going to continue trashing them in the media because it gets huge ratings. Again the message is pounded home that no good deed goes unpunished unless you are exactly who society expects you to be. The alienation that the Turtles experience is so entrenched in society that nothing short of a miracle could change things; the Turtles are profoundly affected by that reality, yet they don't let it mess with their morality or cause them to become cynical. Even living in the very heart of postmodernity, the Turtles do not succumb to its temptations.

As the popularity of the cartoon — and thus of the franchise as a whole — went into decline around the time of the third movie, the series went through a bit of a transformation. Its fans were growing up and becoming less receptive to the often extremely silly plots and characters that were increasingly prevalent in the series. The Turtles had to mutate again. The final three seasons grew darker both figuratively and literally; known as the "Red Sky Episodes," the New York sky was painted a deep red rather than the bright blue it had been in previous seasons. The Turtles finally and definitively defeat Shredder and Krang, and a new villain emerges — an alien called Dregg — along with a new human ally named Carter, who tracks down the Turtles in order to train as a ninja with Master Splinter. The mutagen in the Turtles' bloodstream destabilizes, leading to new and uncontrollable secondary mutations. Despite the retooling, the series was on the descent. After ten years and 196 episodes, its final half-hour, titled "Divide and Conquer," ran in November 1996. A year earlier, the Archie Comics series, spun off from the cartoon, had ended after 72 issues, from August 1988 until October 1995.

A large part of the blame for the cartoon losing steam can be laid at the feet of the Mighty Morphin Power Rangers, the success of which I cannot explain but is probably related to unholy deals with dark forces. *Mighty Morphin Power Rangers* was a show where unconvincing high school students in a fictional California town are granted the power to "morph" (i.e., put on brightly colored bondage suits) and fight people in terrible, campy cardboard-looking monster costumes; when the monster was just about to be defeated, it would grow huge, forcing the Power Rangers to turn into mechanical dinosaurs and then merge into a big stupid robot in order to destroy it. Seriously, that was the plot of *every single episode*. The original fans of the Turtles cartoon had grown up; because the Turtles didn't age in the cartoon, if you were, say, 11 when the first episode premiered, you'd be 17 by '96, older than the Turtles and maybe less into the G-rated cartoon. The darker tone of the retooled show, combined with what seemed like the writers not knowing whether to lean on the series' years of continuity or eschew it altogether, led to some messy storylines that alienated some viewers who had been there from the beginning. The series also failed to appeal to the younger kids who were only now discovering Saturday morning action-oriented television; they were taken in by the bright colors and ineluctable third-act mechanical dinosaurs of *Power Rangers*. The Turtles cartoon had a looser grip on who its audience was, and *Power Rangers* took advantage of that.

While the cartoon was in its death throes, the original comic had a real renaissance. Issue #50 of the Mirage series began the epic, 13-part "City at War" storyline, with Eastman and Laird returning for the first time since 1987. "City at War" saw the Turtles caught between warring factions of the Foot Clan; in the wake of Shredder's (second) death at the Turtles' hands, the clan became divided between Shredder loyalists and those faithful to Karai, the leader of the Foot in Japan who had traveled to New York to get the renegade American franchise back under control. The Turtles enter into a deal with Karai to help her destroy the leaders of the loyalist faction, the Shredder Elite, and in exchange, she vows that under her leadership the Foot will leave the Turtles alone forever, finally allowing them to rest in the wake of the upheaval that they themselves had, in a way, created when they shredded the Shredder all the way back in issue #1.

"City at War" was an archetypal Turtles storyline: action-packed and thoughtful, equal parts bloody and philosophical in the tradition of what made those first issues so compelling and entertaining. It dealt extensively with the themes that made the characters popular in the first place but put them into situations where they were under unprecedented stress. All things changed, yet stayed the same: Splinter, April, and Casey each go on solo adventures to find themselves, during which they confront radical changes, unconventional families, and challenges to their long-held moral principles. At the same time, the four Turtles struggle with growing up and growing apart while being forced to choose sides in a war between factions of the clan they were raised to destroy, a major upheaval that was the direct result of their own actions years ago when they were practically children, blindly following their father's instructions — actions about which they were beginning to feel deeply ambivalent. The sense of disorientation in an increasingly unstable world is also symbolized in a parallel story: an elderly refugee from the then-disintegrating Soviet Union very slowly recovers from injuries sustained when one faction of the Foot Clan bombed a building owned by another faction, a sex shop above which the old man lived in a ratty apartment.

"City at War" concluded with issue #62 and led into the beginning of a new title; *Teenage Mutant Ninja Turtles Volume 2* kicked off in 1993, taking the series in a new direction — and in full color. While the second volume had intriguing stories and fairly beautiful art, sales were unfortunately poor, due to the lagging interest from TMNT's core audience, the plummeting sales of comics in general as a result of the sudden burst of the early '90s speculator market (even mighty Marvel had to declare bankruptcy in 1996), and a very unfortunately timed flood in Massachusetts that destroyed much of Mirage Studios' art, office space, and printing facilities, which disrupted the production schedule. *Volume 2* ran for only 13 issues, ending in October 1995.

A new series, published by Image Comics, started in June 1996, a few months before the end of the cartoon series and less than one year after the end of *TMNT Volume 2*; it was intended to be in the same continuity as the Mirage series.

A little about Image Comics. It was an upstart publisher

created by a few of Marvel's top artists of the time — Rob Liefeld, Todd McFarlane, and Erik Larsen, among others — whose names are today automatic punchlines in the industry and shorthand for hackneyed bullshit among comics readers. But at the time they were lionized for standing up to corporate interests. They staged a coup at Marvel in the name of creator's rights and formed Image Comics. They very nearly brought the entire industry down around them by artificially inflating the market with a seemingly endless parade of gimmicky Collector's Edition comics and progressively more condescendingly brainless storylines that they liked to call "adult." If you think I'm exaggerating, walk into a comic shop sometime and say, "Wow, a first edition copy of *Wetworks* #1!" and make note of the reaction you get. Of course, Marvel and DC had to get in on the action too, and the results were predictably catastrophic.[39]

To be fair, Image is much better now than they used to be — particularly since they started becoming less of a publisher, like Marvel and DC with their stable of artists and writers, and more of a distribution boutique of creator-owned properties that have otherwise nothing to do with Image at all. When *TMNT Volume 3* began, they were already publishing the very excellent Sam Kieth title *The Maxx*, and they went on to put out cool stuff like *Elephantmen*, *Invincible*, and *The Walking Dead*, but they were also publishing the execrable

---

39 Neil Gaiman likened this largely Image-spurred mid '90s comics boom to the 17th century Dutch tulip craze, when such a mania developed for tulips and tulip bulbs that it ended up collapsing the Dutch economy — which also happened to comics, just as Gaiman prophesied.

Savage Dragon and the unavoidable and for a while industry-conquering *Spawn*, for which Todd McFarlane was already co-opting the talents of writers like Alan Moore, Dave Sim, Frank Miller, Grant Morrison, and Neil Gaiman,[40] because he'd apparently completely run out of ideas by issue #7.

The Image Turtles series was most notable for its frequently indecipherable artwork and its use of senseless disfigurement as a surrogate for character development. Within the first five issues, Raphael gets half his face blown off by a robot, and Donatello falls out of a helicopter and is paralyzed and then becomes a cyborg. Later, Leonardo's hand is bitten off by a giant lizard. To mangle a befitting quote from Oscar Wilde: to mutilate one Turtle may be regarded as misfortune; to mutilate three of them looks like carelessness. I got the feeling that the book's creative team[41] did this because they couldn't tell the Turtles apart without initials on their belt buckles. The problem was not the Turtles being violently altered; obviously mutation has always been the characters' bread and butter. It was that the transformations were symbolic of nothing. It was shock value, plain and simple. It was a couple of five-year-olds pulling the legs off ants to make themselves feel powerful.

So that whole thing was crap.

---

40 N.B. Neil Gaiman sued Todd McFarlane in 2002 — and won on all counts — for basically stealing characters that Gaiman had created in the issue of *Spawn* that he wrote. What's especially and bitterly hilarious was the absolute *chutzpah* of McFarlane's defense: that Gaiman's issue of *Spawn* had been work-for-hire and that McFarlane therefore owned all the characters created by Gaiman for the issue and didn't have to pay him any royalties or even acknowledge him as a co-copyright owner. *Which is exactly the kind of slimy disingenuous asshattery that McFarlane et al left Marvel to combat.*

41 And I use the term loosely.

At the same time, there was a live-action TV series on Fox Kids, *Ninja Turtles: The Next Mutation* (1997–1999), and it was equally awful. Because much of the blame for the cancellation of the original TMNT cartoon was attributed to the ascendant *Mighty Morphin Power Rangers*, Saban Entertainment, producer of *Power Rangers*, tried to retool the Turtles to reach that same demographic. The result was disastrous. Not only were the animatronics even worse than in the sub-standard *TMNT III*, but they also bowed to executive pressure and introduced a *fifth turtle* — a female turtle named Venus de Milo, apparently to appeal to girls. Needless to say, this travesty did not succeed. This series also stated that the Turtles were not blood-related, not actually brothers at all, presumably so a possible romance with Venus wouldn't get incesty. Venus was seen as an inauthentic acquiescence to cynical corporate-mandated political correctness, which destroyed the Turtles' brotherly dynamic; written as unrealistically superior to the original Turtles in fighting prowess and overall maturity (because Girl Power™), the character further alienated fans. Also she could do magic. That she was named after a work of art rather than an artist unintentionally belied the fact that she was grossly derivative rather than reverent — a product instead of the result of a creative process. *The Next Mutation* also eschewed practically all the supporting characters and surrounding mythology, and it introduced all-new villains that were as devoid of symbolism and one-dimensional as the cardboard costumes that they wore. Imagine if the second Turtles movie had revealed that Vanilla Ice was their long-lost brother and they spent the whole movie chasing after the scourge of sucka MCs. That's what *The Next Mutation* was like.

There was even a crossover with *Power Rangers* at one point. The whole thing was just unspeakably awful, unpopular with audiences, and loathed by the Turtles' creators; talking about the girl turtle is strictly forbidden among fans, and just mentioning Venus within earshot of Peter Laird is apt to get you punched in the junk. And you would deserve it.

I refer to this period, the three-ish years during which the Image series and *Next Mutation* ran, as the Dark Age of TMNT. Both the Image comic and the live-action show badly misread and misunderstood the Turtles and produced some of the worst garbage in TMNT history. Both these series are widely and rightfully despised by Turtles fans, and both have been officially expunged from the canon by the Turtles' creators. The reason that they were so bad is pretty much this: they both assumed that *nostalgia* for the Turtles would be enough to make them popular, and that just taking what already existed and unnaturally grafting it to what was currently popular with the people whose money they wanted would lead to the kind of success that the original comic and cartoon and movie had enjoyed. A failed and blasphemous Frankensteinian experiment and a crime against nature.

When done right, the Turtles are powerful archetypes with immense storytelling force and cultural resonance. While nostalgia is a component of the formula that makes TMNT compelling, it was not and never could be sufficient on its own. Which is why you can't just go, "It's the Ninja Turtles, except now they're the Power Rangers," and expect anyone to like it. Even fans of the Power Rangers[42] didn't like *The Next Mutation* because it simply didn't work. TMNT owes its adaptability to the immense semiotic strength of its referents — the Frank Miller–esque amalgam of ancient Eastern mysticism with Western sci-fi futurism and the deeply felt yearning for a unique familial covenant that is our sole delivery from inescapable postmodern disaffection. Anything that fails to grok that will fail as a Turtles story, and that's what happened with *Volume 3* and with *The Next Mutation*. By the end of 1999, both of those sad embarrassments were no more. And it was the first time in 15 years, since the first issue of the original comic, that there was no new Ninja Turtles in the world. It was the end of an era.

TMNT lay fallow for the next couple of years. In 2000, Kevin Eastman sold most of his share of the Turtles property to Peter Laird, so that he (Eastman) could focus his attentions on *Heavy Metal*, the borderline-pornographic sci-fi/fantasy comics magazine that had influenced him as a young artist and which he had purchased and been serving as publisher of since 1992. By this point, Eastman and Laird were scarcely on speaking terms anyway.

At the tail end of 2001, the Turtles returned. Peter Laird published the first issue of *TMNT Volume 4* (and the

---

42 Who do exist, for some reason that is, to me, utterly unfathomable.

title actually was the initialism "TMNT" rather than the full "Teenage Mutant Ninja Turtles," probably in the fashion of the very successful relaunch of DC's Justice League of America by writer Grant Morrison, which was simply dubbed *JLA*). *Volume 4* totally ignored the whole Image debacle and took place 15 years after the end of *Volume 2*. The Turtles are older and wiser, and the storyline kicks off with the Utroms arriving on Earth and publicly declaring the existence of extra-terrestrial life to a stunned and largely unprepared humanity. The Utroms ask the people of Earth to assume their place as part of the community of inhabited worlds. Humanity is fairly ambivalent about the idea.

The upshot is that Earth is now lousy with extraterres-trials. It becomes normal to see strange creatures walking around New York City; after all those years of hiding, the Turtles are finally free to wander the streets — everyone just assumes that they're aliens. The symbolism of the increasing integration leading to new freedoms, as well as new threats, is fairly obvious: as the melting pot of America grew increas-ingly diverse, the world of TMNT had to change too, in order for the metaphor to continue to be effective. The Turtles themselves also continued to grow and evolve; they weren't teenagers anymore but young adults, and they were beginning to go their separate ways. Casey Jones and April O'Neil had been married some years before, and their adopted daughter, Shadow, now a teenager, was living with Splinter at Casey's farmhouse in Northampton.

There were problems with pacing (in my opinion, Laird

excels at the kind of high-concept science fiction that *Volume 4* was aiming for, but without Kevin Eastman's more action-oriented sensibility, the overall story dragged in some places); *Volume 4* ran for almost ten years but only 31 issues were published — and it ceased without any sort of resolution at all. We'll get to that.

The point is that Laird used both pastiche and nostalgia to recombine everything from the Turtles' past in order to point them toward the future. There are certain similarities to the Image series that seemed deliberate, to show how to change the Turtles' characters without going for cheap shock value. The bodily transformations that the Turtles suffered in the Image series utterly failed to serve the symbolism that TMNT had used since its beginnings; *Volume 4* was determined to do it right and, in my opinion, it largely succeeded.

The Turtles were getting older, and things were changing. Their beloved teacher and adoptive father, Splinter, dies not in battle but quietly, and alone, in the Northampton farmhouse, of a heart attack. His last, unheard words: "My sons." The death of Splinter and his subsequent and very well-attended funeral (which gave readers a chance to see assembled a great many characters from the Mirage series that we never expected to encounter again) was genuinely one of the most affecting moments in all of TMNT history. How each Turtle dealt with the loss, while at the same time contending with their new freedom and the various complications of their personal lives, made *Volume 4* incredibly bittersweet.

This is where TMNT did nostalgia *right*. There was no

cynical winking at the audience in an attempt to cash in on the remembrance of youth. Just as *Volume 1* used pastiche so effectively as both structure and subject, *Volume 4* did a similar thing with nostalgia: it wasn't just the readers, the fans, who were pining for a time when things were simpler and more fun. The characters were doing the same thing — the Turtles weren't kids anymore, they were physically past their prime, their beloved father was gone, their paths were diverging, and they faced unprecedented challenges, such as the self-proclaimed street army the Madhattan Maulitia, and the pro-human (i.e., anti-alien) terrorist group Xihad (*Volume 4* was very consciously a post-9/11 comic; how could it not have been?), and more personal losses too, like Michelangelo's unexpected anger and sense of betrayal following a one-night stand with an alien dinosaur princess who disappears the next morning without explanation. These are issues that the now-grown-up original fans of the comic related to in the same way that they had related to the franchise years before in its earlier incarnations. Aging, rejection, death, the terror of independence. *Volume 4*'s target audience was the group of fans who had grown up with the Turtles — and were now themselves grown-ups. The comics market itself had by then matured to the point where even mainstream superhero books were consciously being written for *much* older audiences than in decades past.

Around the same time, a new cartoon series began. In 2003, Fox-owned 4Kids TV premiered the second Teenage Mutant Ninja Turtles animated series. It was much closer to the original comic than the 1987 series had been, lifting many plot elements from the Mirage books that had been avoided before. But it was still for children. It was aware of the nostalgia factor and used it to its advantage, but it relegated to Michelangelo much, if not most, of the humor that had been spread across all four Turtles in the first cartoon. The other Turtles respond to his quirks with annoyance. Mikey is the one always down for some pizza, whereas his brothers have more diverse palettes. The first time Michelangelo begins to shout, "Cowabunga," Raphael cuffs him one and tells him to knock it off.

As in the Mirage comics, Splinter was originally a regular rat, and April O'Neil was Baxter Stockman's assistant. Baxter, by the way, was returned to his original race in this series. But the new cartoon also courageously treaded new ground. Perhaps the most controversial story decision was that Shredder was made an Utrom, a criminal named Ch'rell who had crashed and become stranded on Earth (specifically, Japan) hundreds of years ago, who had taken on the identity of Oroku Saki while he attempted to build up the resources to conquer the planet. This shocking twist worked surprisingly well. And the reason it worked, in addition to the high-quality writing, was that despite being very different than everything that had come before, it understood and respected the TMNT canon and how to play around in that world. Following in the pastiche tradition, it combined, in a way, Shredder and Krang from the original cartoon into one character, while making him a member of an alien race that was largely benevolent, as in the Mirage series. It managed to honor its antecedents while remixing them into something new and unexpected.

Some of the other additions to the 2003 series — like Hun, the leader of the Purple Dragons and Shredder's sometimes right-hand man, and the Battle Nexus, an interdimensional arena where the multiverse's greatest warriors come together for a triennial tournament to determine the best fighter in existence[43] — were so well received by audiences and liked by Peter Laird and other writers of the ongoing TMNT books (which now included a second volume of *Tales of the TMNT* that ran for 70 issues) that they actually migrated into the Mirage universe. Hun appeared in some *Tales* issues penned by Tristan Jones, and Leonardo makes his way to the Battle Nexus in the latter part of Peter Laird's *Volume 4*. Which is high praise indeed for the new cartoon.

One episode in particular merits mention, if only to show how genuine this new show was in its investigation of TMNT's overarching theme of physical transformation as symbolic of identity, and how far it was willing to go. Season four's "Insane in the Membrane" never aired; the network deemed it too horrifying. One can see their point. The episode featured Baxter Stockman cloning a new body for himself, after his original body had been progressively mutilated by Shredder as punishment for Baxter's numerous failures, eventually rendering him no more than a brain and a single

---

43 Previous champions include Hamato Yoshi, the Shredder, Splinter, and eventually . . . Michelangelo! A fact of which Mikey never fails to remind Raphael if Raph's teasing of him gets a little out of hand.

eyeball floating in a jar. That's not the horrifying bit. Baxter transplants his brain into the new cloned body, which begins to slowly decompose over the course of the episode. It wasn't only the graphic decomposition of Baxter's form that led to the episode being banned from television — although at one point when his jaw falls off and he has to reattach it, it's . . . uh, really, really gross. The faulty clone leads Baxter to experience uncontrollable memory flashbacks, where we learn that his villainy is the result of being raised by a physically and emotionally distant mother and of an overpowering sense of guilt that, even with all his scientific genius, he was unable to save his mother from some horrible wasting disease. Pretty heavy for a kids show, right?

Unfortunately, the 2003 series went more than slightly off the rails. In its sixth season, the show was rebranded, the characters somewhat redesigned, and the Turtles were pulled 100 years into the future. Now called *Teenage Mutant Ninja Turtles: Fast Forward*, it became much more kiddy and jokey. It betrayed the established tone of the series, which had received laurels for successfully balancing the seriousness of its source material with the lighter requirements of a show meant for children. And when longtime viewers were six years older than they'd been when the series premiered, the show started courting kids who were much younger. It was similar in intent, though opposite in direction, as the retooling that the original cartoon series had undergone in its latter days, and it fared similarly. Luckily, this silliness didn't last long; *Fast Forward*'s reception was poor, and after one season the Turtles were returned to their proper era. The rest of the series, retitled *Teenage Mutant Ninja Turtles: Back to the Sewers*, returned to its action-packed atmosphere and continued until its absolutely triumphant feature-length series finale in 2009. Its seven seasons didn't match the then-unprecedented decade-long run of its predecessor, but it was still pretty impressive.

In 2007, 14 years after the last Turtles film, Imagi Entertainment produced a new TMNT movie — called *TMNT*, like the ongoing Mirage comic. It was fully rendered in CGI, intended as a continuation of the movie series that had left off in 1993.

Reviews were mixed, but most criticized it for not being enough like the 1987 cartoon — i.e., for not catering enough to nostalgia. In the *Toronto Star*, Peter Howell lamented that "[Writer-director Kevin] Munroe seeks to stoke the nostalgia flames of the original comic book fans, who are now in their 30s, while at the same time reaching out to younger new fans. He fails on both counts, because the movie is neither clever enough for adults nor compelling enough for kids." Richard Roeper (of Ebert and Roeper) wrote, "I guess if you read the comic strip and you played the video games and you watched the TV show and dug the earlier movies, you'll dig this new version. For me, I didn't do any of that stuff," implying that there was nothing enjoyable there for anyone besides the nostalgianauts. However, I think that *TMNT* is the second best of the Turtles movies, just barely falling short of the first film. And here's why: in stark contrast to *The Next Mutation*, also ostensibly a sequel to the movie series, *TMNT* honored everything that came before it. Nostalgia *was* one factor — this is made most explicit in a scene at the end of the movie where we're shown artifacts symbolizing the first three movies, including Shredder's helmet, the TCRI ooze canister, and the Time Scepter — but like Peter Laird's *Volume 4*, it also developed the metaphor in its narrative. When the movie begins, the team has been fractured: Donatello works as a computer tech-support phone line operator, Michelangelo entertains children at birthday parties (wearing a giant foam replica of his head over his real head), Raphael (unbeknownst to the rest of the Turtles) is fighting crime at night encased in metal armor as the Nightwatcher, and Leonardo has been gone for an entire year, training his skills in South America. As their family fragments, even their individual identities take a hit as they must go even deeper into hiding, just as they attempt to find a place in the world when their lives, without the threat of Shredder and the Foot Clan to fight, are suddenly devoid of meaning. The four reassemble when the Foot Clan reappears, under the leadership of Karai, while eccentric billionaire Max Winters assembles an army of monsters for unknown but presumably nefarious reasons.

The cast was almost unbelievably impressive. April O'Neil was voiced by Sarah Michelle Gellar (*Buffy the Vampire Slayer*); Casey Jones was played by Chris Evans (the future Captain America); Zhang Ziyi (*Crouching Tiger, Hidden Dragon*) portrayed Karai; Laurence Fishburne voiced the opening narration (which is the only totally extraneous piece of the movie, but still); and big bad Max Winters was played by none other than Sir Patrick Stewart, Officer of the Order of the British Empire. Kevin Smith (director of *Clerks*) had a cameo as a restaurant cook, and Splinter was played by screen and voice acting veteran of nearly 50 years Mako Iwamatsu — his first movie role was in 1959, and *TMNT* was his very last film before his death in 2006 at age 72.

Again like *Volume 4* of the Mirage comic, the film's theme was about growing up and learning how to remain a family while individuating oneself. Even Casey and April are going through some stuff; at one point Casey and Raph have a late-night talk where Casey admits he's worried about his relationship with April, saying, "I don't know if I can be the grown-up she needs me to be."

The ever-present tension between Leonardo and Raphael comes to a head when an argument (Raphael is furious at Leonardo for "abandoning" the team; Leo insists he did it *for* the team, in order to learn to be a better leader) erupts into an intense, out-and-out brawl between the two brothers. The Leo-versus-Raph fight is one of the most spectacular scenes in the history of the franchise, if you ask me. The battle, on a rooftop before the New York City skyline and in the midst of a near-torrential downpour, is gorgeously animated and powerfully choreographed. The anger as well as the love between the two brothers is palpable onscreen, the stakes are high for both characters, and their crisis feels painfully genuine.

TMNT was reasonably successful at the box office, making

$95 million with a $35 million budget and taking the top spot in its opening weekend, deposing the Zack Snyder–directed adaptation of Frank Miller's historical-fantasy indie comic based on the Battle of Thermopylae, *300* (which is a bit of an interesting coincidence), and planning began for a sequel. Meanwhile, Mirage's *Volume 4* was in trouble; Peter Laird was taking longer and longer between issues, finding it difficult to keep up the pace — because his toning and inking skills were slowing down with age, and due to his waning enthusiasm and difficulties in his personal life. Turtles fatigue, for the second time in two decades, was threatening to set in.

The feature-length series finale of the second Turtles cartoon was broadcast in fall 2009. "Turtles Forever" was nothing less than a love letter to 25 years of Ninja Turtles fandom and a powerful metaphor for the cultural significance of the entire TMNT transmedia franchise, as well as a hell of a great adventure on its own terms. And I'm going to throw in a spoiler warning here for anyone who hasn't seen it; it's just so good that I hate to ruin all its amazing twists. But I will.

We open with the Turtles watching a news report about an attempted robbery by the Purple Dragons that was seemingly foiled by the Turtles themselves, except they had nothing to do with it. When they head out to investigate, what they find is . . . the Turtles from the 1987 cartoon! In all their silly glory, initials on their belt buckles and everything. We learn that, back in the 1987 world, the Turtles were battling Shredder in the Technodrome when the dimensional portal malfunctioned, apparently pulling the Turtles — and, as it turns out, the Technodrome itself, along with Shredder, Krang, Bebop, and Rocksteady — into this alternate universe with its own versions of the Turtles. When 1987 Shredder learns what's happened, he goes searching for his 2003-world duplicate — and discovers Ch'rell, the Utrom Shredder who has been frozen in ice deep in space. Once Ch'rell is reanimated, he decides to use the advanced (but ridiculous) technology of Dimension-X to destroy the Turtles forever.

The parallel universe thing is a fairly common trope in science fiction, but something slightly and intriguingly different is going on here. The two sets of Ninja Turtles aren't just from arbitrary different worlds; they're from worlds that we, the audience, already know. As a plot device, the multiverse concept is a great way for the audience to indulge in some nostalgia and to highlight the contrasts between the 1987 series' lighthearted, kid-friendly tone and the more serious, darker spirit of the 2003 series. But there's a lot more going on too. The way that the story unfolds reveals some deep truths about how and why TMNT has managed to stick around long enough to be simultaneously relevant and nostalgic, and adaptable as ever.

At the end of act two of "Turtles Forever," Ch'rell, having built himself frightening new armor, taken over and remodeled the Technodrome into a crazy, CGI Death Star–looking thing, and styled himself as "the One, True Shredder," has captured both Turtles teams and strapped them into an enormous centrifuge connected to the dimensional portal generator.

He explains that this dimension is only a single world in a seemingly endless multiverse. Like branches on a tree, he says, each dimension sprang from a common source: different in many ways but similar at the core. In each of these different worlds, there's a version of the Teenage Mutant Ninja Turtles who always stop that world's version of the Shredder. Ch'rell uses the portal to show the Turtles — and the audience — images of the countless variations of them that exist throughout the multiverse. What we see are portraits from the various iterations of the Turtles across 25 years and every imaginable medium: comic books, live action, animation (traditional cell-animated as well as computer-generated), video games, and so on.[44]

Shredder's goal is to locate the "source dimension," whence all versions of the Turtles originate; "destroy the source," he says, "and you would set off a chain reaction that would destroy Ninja Turtles everywhere, forevermore!"

The source dimension, we discover (after Karai, realizing that Shredder's plan would not just destroy the Turtles but wipe out the entire multiverse, sabotages the dimensional analyzer and saves the Turtles), is Kevin Eastman and Peter Laird's original black-and-white comic from 1984, and the multiverse of "Turtles Forever" is a metafictional analog for the multimedia empire of Teenage Mutant Ninja Turtles. We

---

44 Conspicuously absent are any shots from the Image comic series or *The Next Mutation*, both best forgotten.

get to watch as the two Turtle teams follow the Technodrome back to the source dimension, where they meet up with a third quartet of Turtles — the original, grim and gritty monochrome mutants from Mirage issue #1.

It's pretty epic.

There's actually some complicated narratology going on in "Turtles Forever," aside from its grand-scale awesomeness. Not only does it acknowledge the nostalgia factor head-on,[45] the storyline's execution is very meta without quite breaking the fourth wall;[46] it's a brilliant sort of compare-and-contrast analysis of what makes TMNT so radical. A lot of that is stuff we've discussed here already, but there are a couple of other points that "Turtles Forever" raises that we should go into before closing this major chapter of the franchise's history.

From the very beginning, TMNT has been deeply intertextual. By using pastiche to make hybridity both its structure and its subject, TMNT was the kind of art that was enjoyable on its own merits but also revealed its inner workings by rewarding readers who were familiar with its references — a thoroughly postmodern storytelling style. We already know that. But by the time we get to "Turtles Forever" a full quarter century later, that intertextuality is so much denser and that

---

45 When the 1984 Turtles call the 2003 Turtles "sellouts" for having different-colored bandanas, 2003 Raphael tries to save face by pointing out that the 1987 Turtles have their initials on their belt buckles — a really clever little shout-out to the old-school Turtle fans who've criticized every incarnation of the TMNT other than the Mirage series for being too watered-down and childish.

46 Besides the couple of times that 1987 Raphael addresses the camera, which is something that occasionally happened in their series so it doesn't really count. Hun, at one point, makes note of this, patching up the fourth wall with the outburst: "Who are you talking to? There's no one there!"

much more rewarding. Because of the generation-spanning culture that's built up around Ninja Turtles, every new work in the Turtles multiverse comprises all the other previous stories and prior incarnations. That's why the nostalgia around Ninja Turtles works in quite a different way than it does for lots of other cultural artifacts — it's not only that feeling you get remembering what it was like to wake up one Saturday morning in 1990 to find that you had *two* brand new episodes of Turtles coming at you instead of just one. It's that echo of everything you know about the whole history of Turtles in every new manifestation of TMNT. Inside your head, there's a map just like the one inside Shredder's dimensional scanner, a diagram of the Turtleverse that lights up in various locations when you see a canister of glowing ooze or recall the timeless aphorism that "Turtles fight with honor."

It's a fundamental component of our postmodern culture that everything is intimately interconnected, and any media production invariably reconfigures the whole. The Turtles franchise proves — in "Turtles Forever" more explicitly than in any other Turtles story before or since — that it's got a super sophisticated reader model going on. Pastiche and nostalgia are both inherently intertextual tropes, and Turtles uses them to the full extent of the law, as it were, deploying them as storytelling devices as well as engines for philosophical and metafictional inquiry. Because the transmedia franchise in general, and TMNT in particular, is never simply a number of isolated products but an ongoing conversation between creators, media, and audience and we all know it, it would be dumb and borderline dishonest not to make that part of the narrative. We'd notice that it was missing.[47]

"Turtles Forever" ends on an appropriately nostalgic yet genuinely funny and touching note. After defeating Shredder and saving the multiverse (of course), the Turtles are all returned to their own worlds. We linger in the black-and-white 1984 Mirage universe, where the prototypical Turtles leap from a rooftop and the action freezes on a striking pose from that first comic book as a voiceover from a caption from that issue declares, "We are the Teenage Mutant Ninja Turtles. We strike hard and fade away . . . into the night."

Pull back to reveal the actual original art for that page, and suddenly we switch to a live-action shot of Eastman and Laird's studio, pencil drawings for the first comic strewn all about, and Kevin Eastman and Peter Laird (the real Eastman and Laird lending their voices for the scene) deciding to take a break from drawing to go get some pizza; Kevin cheerfully says, "Boy, I sure hope this thing sells." To which Peter, laughing, responds, "Yeah, I was thinking the same thing."

Not a dry eye in the house, I'm telling you.

A beautiful bookend to the Second Age of the Turtles, even more poignant in retrospect. Nobody could have known it at the time, but "Turtles Forever" would be the final Turtles

---

47 I think this is one of the reasons that the Star Wars prequels were so bad overall. They failed to navigate adroitly all the accumulated paratext (the "Expanded Universe") between *Return of the Jedi* (1983) and *The Phantom Menace* (1999). While it's not necessary to maintain *everything* as canonical, ejecting the narratively sagacious interconnections drawn by the franchise's many tie-in novels, comics, games, etc., in favor of seemingly arbitrary allusions just felt insulting. It's also a big part of why the Image Turtles series and *The Next Mutation* sucked cloaca.

work in the world's most successful indie art empire. The first episode of the 2003 series was entitled "Things Change," and it would be wise always to remember that, because after this finale, capping off two influential cartoons and turning the page (both literally and figuratively) on the culture-shaking comic book, Teenage Mutant Ninja Turtles would never again be the same.

4

Remixed and Reincarnated

NINJA TURTLES SNAPPED UP BY NICKELODEON

NEW YORK (*Hollywood Reporter*) — Viacom's Nickelodeon has acquired the global rights to the Teenage Mutant Ninja Turtles kids' entertainment franchise from the Mirage Group and 4Kids Entertainment for approximately $60 million.

It unveiled plans Wednesday to develop a new CG-animated TV series based on the franchise, expected to premiere in 2012, and a new feature film in partnership with Viacom's Paramount Pictures unit, also planned for 2012.

The company's goal is to reintroduce the

25-year-old franchise, centered on a quartet of crime-fighting turtles, to existing and potential new fans.

The deal also gives Nickelodeon all merchandising rights. It will continue to work with the franchise's long-term toy partner, Playmates Toys.

The world woke up one morning to find that Peter Laird had sold Teenage Mutant Ninja Turtles to Nickelodeon, owned by MTV, owned by Viacom. The characters and stories we loved, that had started out as a self-published indie comic and gone on to overrun the entire world for the next 25 years were now a wholly owned property of a faceless multinational media conglomerate. Nobody saw it coming, and we just didn't know what to think.

It was an unexpected event, but apparently it had been a long time coming. Kevin Eastman hadn't been part of the franchise for years by the time of the sale in 2009, and though Peter Laird had been fairly heavily involved in the 2003 cartoon and had been writing and inking the *TMNT Volume 4* comic, the truth was his interest was waning. Each issue took longer to arrive than the last, and they were selling less and less. Toward the end of its run, it wasn't even available at comic shops, only by direct order through Mirage. Its final issue was nothing more than a bunch of jpgs Laird posted on his website.

The sale to Nickelodeon shocked fans and caused not a little outrage. One of the things we appreciated about TMNT was that, since its very beginning, it had been *independent*. It was created by these two guys, not by some corporate culture factory. And that independent spirit was part of its very ethos. TMNT's success was a major force in strengthening creator's rights, which allowed comics creators to live on their own terms rather than being indentured servants of Marvel and DC. And throughout everything, though Eastman and Laird had given up more and more of the day-to-day responsibility for what happened in the Turtles' world to others, the creators still had the final word.

But not anymore. On his blog, Peter Laird explained that the Turtles had taken up the majority of his time for the past 25 years — almost half of his life. Not only that, but dealing with the business side of things had worn him down, given him precious little time to work on his art and little reason to be excited about it — which was the reason he got into comics in the first place. Finally, he realized the toll that the success of TMNT had taken on his family life. Late one night, he was working on the computer when it occurred to him that he couldn't remember the last time that he had gone to bed at the same time as his wife. He'd begun to feel like he was neglecting his family — and he didn't want to be that guy.

So when Nickelodeon came knocking, with enthusiasm, exciting plans, and 60 million dollars, Peter Laird did what he thought was the right thing. When you look at it from his point of view, it's hard to think badly of the guy.

That said — what would become of our Teenage Mutant Ninja Turtles? Would they thrive under this new regime, or would they suffer? Would Viacom/MTV/Nickelodeon entrust the property to writers and artists who understood what the Turtles were all about, and who could bring them to a new generation while keeping them rooted to their origins? Or would they milk the nostalgia for all it was worth just to make as much money as possible, and to hell with authenticity?

The fact that it was Nickelodeon that bought TMNT gave me some hope. Nick had been known as one of the major forces in excellent and sometimes groundbreaking animation for quite a while. *The Ren & Stimpy Show*, created by John Kricfalusi, was a revelation in 1991 with its bizarre comedy, unique art style, and originality of character design. In 1999, Nick premiered *Spongebob Squarepants*, the adorable and bizarre underwater adventures of the inhabitants of Bikini Bottom, which was also awesome and hilarious, straight up to the theatrical release of *The Spongebob Squarepants Movie* in 2004, which was *amazing* (and included parts for Alec Baldwin as an aquatic assassin, Scarlett Johansson as the Princess of the Ocean, and David Hasselhoff as himself). Then there was *Invader Zim*, created by Jhonen Vasquez, writer/artist behind the big-deal indie comic *Johnny the Homicidal Maniac*. Zim, an alien from the planet Irk, where social status directly correlates with height, is exiled to Earth to keep him from ruining the Irken Empire's plot for galactic conquest with his boundless enthusiasm and equally boundless incompetence. And in 2005, Nickelodeon produced *Avatar: The Last Airbender*, an Asian-influenced but American-created series praised for its complex storytelling and magical-mythological overtones. It ran for three seasons, ending when its creators wanted it to rather than dragging on endlessly because it was still making money — which was a good sign.[48]

The point is, there was reason to hope that Nickelodeon would do the Turtles right.

As the new cartoon went into production, it was announced that a new series of TMNT comics would be produced by IDW Publishing. Another good sign: an indie publisher that was producing some of the best licensed titles out there today, IDW's books included Doctor Who, Transformers, Ghostbusters, G.I. Joe, and Star Trek, massive properties that have all been done justice by the writers and artists working on them, even in cases where the big-budget theatrical counterpart was an insulting assemblage of mechanical abortions.[49] When IDW announced that the new series would be co-plotted by Kevin Eastman, that was another win for the good guys. The IDW series kicked off in August 2011, and while it had a radically new take on the Turtles' origin and suffered from some pacing problems out of the gate, overall I have to say that it's succeeding, and here's why.

In this universe, the Turtles and Splinter were subjects of animal testing at StockGen, a high-tech company owned by, of course, Baxter Stockman, who has allied himself with Krang, a brutal warlord from Dimension X whose own homeworld has been destroyed and who plans to conquer Earth to use as his

---

48 In 2010, a live-action movie based on the series, called *The Last Airbender* and directed by M. Night Shyamalan, came out and was a horrible disaster.

49 I'm looking at you, Michael Bay's *Transformers*.

new base of operations for the dimensional war he is prosecuting. April O'Neil is a college student interning at StockGen, who named the four turtles after her favorite Renaissance artists. When members of the Foot Clan break into StockGen one night to steal the valuable alien chemicals stored there, Splinter and the Turtles are exposed to the mutagen and escape, eventually transforming into their new humanoid bodies.

But how did Splinter and the Turtles gain their personalities and their ninja skills? It turns out that they are the *reincarnations* of Hamato Yoshi and his four young sons, who lived in feudal Japan and were murdered by Yoshi's rival, Oroku Saki. Their souls transmigrated into animal bodies centuries later, then were reborn yet again when they came into contact with the mutagen. While Splinter retains most of his memories of his life as Hamato Yoshi, the Turtles can recall barely anything about theirs, though their fighting abilities (and favorite colors) remain intact.

This is a pretty big shift from the original backstory. And it's a little hard to swallow at first — even Donatello, in the comic, fairly berates Leonardo for suggesting it at one point. And yet the reincarnation angle kind of works even at the start, and it makes more and more sense as things go along, and there are two major reasons for that. First, it nicely solves the problem of how Splinter, a regular rat, could have become a ninja master prior to his mutation, which is something that every version of TMNT has had to deal with at one point or another.

The other thing, which is brilliantly subtle, is that the reincarnation element hearkens back to TMNT's real beginnings, all the way back to Frank Miller's *Ronin*, where the rebirth of an ancient masterless samurai in futuristic New York City is the book's most basic premise. Which is to say that IDW didn't make such a major change to the characters' origin simply to be shocking or to put their own stamp on it; they did it because it was true to TMNT's artistic origins and the spirit of pastiche that informed the Turtles' creation in the first place. It also opens up whole new storytelling possibilities, as the IDW TMNT miniseries *Secret History of the Foot Clan* (one of the high points of the series thus far) proves.

At the same time, IDW has not been shy to use characters from the entire gamut of Turtles history — we've seen the Fugitoid from the Mirage comics fighting alongside the Neutrinos from the 1987 cartoon, for instance. And of course there are new characters as well, like the mutant alley cat Old Hob and the arctic fox Alopex. There have been a handful of excellent, classic-quality Turtles stories coming out of IDW since the new series' advent. Besides the aforementioned *Secret History of the Foot Clan*, there was the TMNT micro-series, which followed in the footsteps of Mirage's single-issue adventure for each Turtle early in the run; there was the two-part *Infestation* event, a company-wide crossover wherein multiple titles had to contend with an invasion of Lovecraftian horrors (*Infestation: Teenage Mutant Ninja Turtles* was written by Mirage-ite Tristan Jones and was genuinely great both as a Turtles story and as Lovecraft fanfic); and topping off that first year of IDW's TMNT was *Teenage Mutant Ninja Turtles Annual 2012*, a 48-page comic written and drawn entirely by

Kevin Eastman, who hadn't done a complete Turtles book since 1992, a full 20 years earlier.[50]

A few months after the debut of the IDW comic book series, the new cartoon premiered on Nicktoons. It was entirely computer-generated and came with its own changes — some obvious, some less so, and some entirely cosmetic but nevertheless controversial. In this version, Splinter is once again originally Hamato Yoshi, the human ninja master whose life and family was rent apart by Oroku Saki (not only was Yoshi's wife, Tang Shen, killed by the Shredder in this version, but he also had a young daughter, who he presumes was also murdered . . .). After fleeing to New York City, Yoshi is one day going home after buying four baby turtles from a pet store, and he follows a suspicious-looking man carrying a strange glowing canister. When Yoshi is discovered, a fight breaks out; the canister is smashed and Yoshi and the turtles are exposed to the glowing ooze inside . . . you can probably see where this is going.

April O'Neil is a high school student here, of an age with the Turtles themselves. For the first time, the Turtles are significantly physically distinct from each other — some past versions had their skin various shades of green to distinguish them a little, but here, they're different heights (Donnie's the tallest, followed by Leo, Raph, and then Mikey); Donatello

50 Reading *TMNT Annual* felt like coming home again — although I think it could have used some of Peter Laird's logical grounding to rein it in a bit here and there; Eastman's storytelling style is very fast and loose, and it works great in bursts, but 48 pages of it does get kind of exhausting. The story of two rival gangs of ninjas, badass New York City street gangs, and Raphael and Casey Jones getting stuck in the middle was funny, dynamic, and brutal, and Kevin Eastman's art hasn't declined even a little bit since the good old days.

has a small gap between his front two teeth; Raphael has some pretty serious battle damage on his shell and plastron; and Mike has *freckles*. After a number of comics and the 2007 movie had been meditations on growing older in a world that was itself aging, rebooting the Turtles into much younger incarnations was a bold move directed at recapturing the interest of fun-loving but probably alienated children. And you know, I'm okay with that. It's clever, it's appropriate, and it works. Way better than giving them random disfigurements. The Turtles in this version are more childlike than in any previous incarnation — and not in a bad way. They're often impetuous, they try hard to live up to Splinter's high expectations, and they get their butts kicked more often than not. Not that they aren't fierce fighters, but they also frequently find themselves outmatched — and when they can't outfight or outsmart their enemies, they have to retreat. It happens more often than you'd expect. But they also *learn* from their defeats, mainly through Splinter's loving yet sometimes harsh guidance. Basically, they feel like a family trying to find their place in the world. As they should.

Despite all the changes, you can see how devoted the show's creators are to their artistic predecessors of the franchise in the opening theme song. Now, you remember the original Turtles theme. I know you do. It's one of the best, if not *the* best cartoon theme song of all time — right up there with Spider-Man doing whatever a spider can. It's high energy and catchy as hell, and it was written by Chuck Lorre, who went on to create NBC's popular sitcom *The Big Bang Theory*. The 2003 cartoon had its own theme song . . . which was really pretty bad. The 2012 series did exactly what they should have done with their theme song: they remixed and updated the original.

We open in deep space, zoom in fast to Earth, New York City, a manhole cover. The familiar strains of "Teenage Mutant Ninja Turtles . . . heroes in a half shell . . . Turtle Power!" So far so good. We're in well-trod territory here. But when we get to the verse, it's a whole new ballgame. Over the beat we hear hard-hitting rap a bit reminiscent of "T.U.R.T.L.E. Power," which played over the end credits of the first Turtles movie. The stanzas introduce us to each turtle in the very same order as in the original cartoon's song, with visuals showcasing each one's fighting skills — and showing off the very impressive feats of CGI going on in the show. There's a shout-out to *The Secret of the Ooze*, the second Turtles movie. The intro is silly and badass at the same time, which is exactly the right tone, and the final pose that the Turtles strike is the very same one on the cover of *TMNT Volume 1*, issue #1.

You watch this opening and you go, *These dudes have done their homework.*

And that pretty much persists through the whole show. Besides the prodigious voice talents of Jason Biggs (*American Pie*) as Leonardo, Sean Astin (*Lord of the Rings*) as Raphael, Rob Paulsen (who played Raphael in the original cartoon!) as Donatello, Greg Cipes (most famous as the voice of Beast Boy in the *Teen Titans* animated series and — get this — a professional surfer! How perfect is that?) as Michelangelo, and Mae Whitman (*Arrested Development*, *Scott Pilgrim vs. the World*,

Parenthood) as April, the storylines and characters are well balanced between brand-new stuff and stuff lifted out of previous incarnations and adapted to their new circumstances.

For instance, we have the brain-like creatures stranded on Earth that run T.C.R.I. and created the mutagen — but they're not the benevolent Utroms of the original comic; they're a malevolent species looking to transform Earth into a copy of their home planet, which is in another universe called Dimension X, and the race is called the Kraang. Instead of Bebop and Rocksteady, Shredder's new pair of hench mutants are Chris Bradford, owner and operator of a famous national chain of dojos (and a thinly disguised homage to Chuck Norris), and Xever, an ex–gang member and master of the Brazilian martial art capoeira. They're eventually mutated, of course; Bradford becomes a ten-foot-tall Akita dog, while Xever transforms into a fish (probably a Giant Snakehead) with a venomous bite, who needs specially constructed cybernetic legs and apparatus to breathe outside water. Michelangelo nicknames them Dogpound and Fishface, respectively.[51]

One big controversial difference between the new Nick TMNT and all previous versions is that these Turtles have *three* toes instead of only two. I'm really not sure what that's all about.

The first episode of the new TMNT series was the highest-rated kids' show on basic cable that week and Nickelodeon's top-rated premiere for an animated show since 2009, with 3.9

---

51 Mikey's dubbing new characters with terrible punning nicknames is a kind of running joke throughout the show; after encountering Xever in his newly mutated form, Mike calls him Fishface and Leo, laughing incredulously, says, "You're calling him Fishface?" Mikey responds, "It was either that, or Robocarp."

million viewers in the U.S. It was so well received that it was renewed for a second season after just one episode had aired. Then less than four months later, a third season was ordered. That's the good news. Here's the bad news.

Plans for a new Turtles movie were also underway. The first thing we learned was that Michael Bay's production company, Platinum Dunes, was going to be producing it. This did not create a lot of optimism among the Turtle-loving community, because Michael Bay's movies are widely seen as being stupid and awful, thanks to abominable dreck such as *Transformers* and *Pearl Harbor*.

Those of us reluctant to abandon all hope immediately rationalized: Bay isn't *directing* it. He's not *writing* it. He's just putting up the money. It could still be good. Then it was announced that the screenplay would be directed by Jonathan Liebesman, of *Battle: Los Angeles* and *Wrath of the Titans* infamy. And then we learned that the title of the movie would be the truncated *Ninja Turtles*, and certain comments from Michael Bay indicated that the Turtles would be "from an alien race." While the fandom was trying to figure out what that was supposed to mean — hoping against hope that it was simply a reference to the extraterrestrial origin of the mutagen — the script leaked.

Written by Josh Appelbaum and André Nemec (who worked on the TV series *Alias* and the movie *Mission Impossible: Ghost Protocol*, which, okay), the screenplay, nicknamed "The Blue Door," was . . . how can I even describe it? Oh, I know: an *atrocity*. A crime against God and man. And turtle. I'm not prepared to say it was *worse* than genocide. But it wasn't any *better*.

Of all its many, many flaws, the most egregious was this: the Turtles and Splinter were *aliens*. Not mutants. Aliens. From a planet full of humanoid turtles. This, to put it gently, was the worst idea in the history of human endeavor. And I'm sure you can understand why. It undermines the whole basic metaphor of the Turtles. The negotiation of hybridized identity in a postmodern world is the entire point, and removing the *mutant* from the Teenage Mutant Ninja Turtles strips them of all the social relevance and cultural resonance that made the characters so compelling in the first place. Alien Turtles is the product of a mind that clearly has no grasp of who the Turtles are or what has made them so great and cool for the past three decades.

It's the world's response to this harrowing pronouncement that's almost more interesting than the blasphemous news was itself. What happened is that the universe exploded. It wasn't just the ever-querulous Turtles nerds like me who were deploring the desecration of our sacred text and reprimanding this heretic, entreating heaven for the immediate cessation of all his biological processes and consignment of his soul to the eternal abyss, alone and unmourned, his forsaken mortal remains interred, preferably, in the middle of the night at some undisclosed aquatic location so the site couldn't become a shrine for those poor confused proselytes of *Bad Boys II*.

No, *everybody* was pissed off about this. Mainstream entertainment news sources picked it up and the comments sections of sites all across this Internet we call Internet ran crimson with blood. People who literally had not thought about Ninja Turtles for 20 years were paroxysmic at the idea of the Turtles being aliens instead of mutants. Now of course it's not like *The Onion AV Club* is exactly known for being equanimity headquarters, but you see the point I'm trying to make. Even non-fans, people who generally did not give a barf about Ninja Turtles, realized that taking the *M* out of *TMNT* was the stupidest shit ever and avowed that they'd have no truck with such a senseless contrivance. I'm pretty sure the U.N. called an emergency meeting of the Security Council. Anyone even remotely familiar with the property instinctually understood what Michael Bay didn't, or couldn't, or wouldn't: that mutation and mutantness — *transformation* — is the most essential component of the whole Turtles thing, what makes it resonant and meaningful.

And perhaps the most incredible part of all this outrage? *Michael Bay blinked.*

Next thing you know, Bay comes out to insist that "the leaked script for Ninja Turtles that different sites continue to comment on was written well before I, or anyone at Platinum Dunes, was involved with the project. That script saw the shredder[52] long ago." Which is a *blatant lie*, because the script was dated January 30, 2012, and Platinum Dunes signed on in May 2010.[53]

---

52 Nice one, Michael. I see what you did there.

53 He later tried to explain this away by saying that completing the actual deal took years — but since the script had leaked less than six months after the date printed on it, how "well before" could it really have been?

Suddenly the word was that *Ninja Turtles* production had been delayed for ten months so a new script could be written. Later on, it was announced that the title had been changed back to *Teenage Mutant Ninja Turtles*. Conspiracy theories proliferated: did Bay, suspecting that this aliens thing might not go over very well, leak the script deliberately as a sort of test screening to see which way the wind would blow before beginning the (very expensive) shooting process? Or was he just trolling us, like when he announced that Megatron was not going to be in *Transformers 2*, even though Megatron was totally in *Transformers 2*? Or was the leak just a coincidence, but being the savvy businessman that Bay is, he realized that the movie he was planning to make simply would not play and made a last-minute decision to go back to the drawing board?

We just don't know, and those of us on the outside will probably never know what transpired between the first pitch meeting and the final product. Maybe that's for the best. But whatever your opinion on what ends up onscreen — and the opinions of dyed-in-the-wool Turtles fans and someone who happens to stumble into the cinema to see *New Movie Out This Weekend* are likely to be incongruent with each other — the backlash proved that the built-in audience and pretty much 100 percent of the *potential* audience hated the idea of the Turtles not being mutants. And this was a meaningful event. Teenage Mutant Ninja Turtles succeeds because *we get it* and *it gets us*. When you put someone in charge who can't relate, who doesn't understand hybridization because they are paid to be an insider and appeal to the well-adjusted masses . . . well, let's just say that things go wrong.[54]

At this sensitive moment, the wisdom of Master Splinter himself comes to mind. Allow me to paraphrase from the climactic scene of the first Teenage Mutant Ninja Turtles film, the unsurpassed pinnacle of live-action TMNT adaptations, whence we all may learn:

Death comes for us all, Michael Bay. But something much worse comes for you. For when *you* die, it will be *without honor.*

---

54 ATTN: Mr. Hieronymous P. Viacom, Esq.
Subject: TMNT

Dear Mr. Viacom,

By now you have realized the error of your ways. In all likelihood, as you read this, it is around three in the morning and you are in your office, sitting at your favorite desk, the one carved from the remains of the astronomical object that so many years ago precipitated the extinction of the dinosaurs, and you are contemplating whether to reach for your next highball of Ketel One and Hellman's or into the bottom drawer, beneath all those back issues of *Variety* from the 1970s that you had specially bronzed like baby shoes, for the loaded pearl-handled revolver you keep hidden in case of entertainment emergencies.

Yes, Mr. Viacom. I know about the bottom drawer.

Listen carefully. You don't have to keep doing this. It is not too late to save yourself. I only want what is best for you. I am here to *help* you. *I will write you the next Ninja Turtles movie.* I will write it *for free.*

I am totally serious. I will write it and it will be the best Ninja Turtles movie ever. Not because I am some genius** — there are thousands of people out there who could write the best Ninja Turtles movie ever; God knows that Guillermo del Toro or Edgar Wright or (dare I even dream?) Joss Whedon would do it 74 million times better than I ever could — but because I am a person who knows the Turtles, understands the Turtles, has lived with the Turtles for the majority of his conscious life. Because I am a person who cares, genuinely and profoundly, about Teenage Mutant Ninja Turtles, as if they were my very own brothers. And that, Mr. Viacom, is what the Turtles deserve. Somebody who cares about them. They would do the same for you. You know that they would.

Put down that gun, Mr. Viacom. And pick up that phone.

With all due respect,

Richard Rosenbaum
c/o ECW Press
Toronto, Canada

* Plus 2.5 gross points on the back-end. I mean, I'm not an idiot.
** Though if the MacArthur Foundation sees the film and chooses to make a one-time exception for Canadian citizens, who am I to argue?

5

Turtles All the Way Down

In his book *Convergence Culture*, media scholar Henry Jenkins traces the contemporary relationship between creators, audiences, and the media back to Star Wars, citing it as the archetypal cultural object that broke the barrier between the commercial entertainment industry and grassroots folk culture, enriching them both. And he's right; Star Wars did a lot to inspire what Pierre Lévy called knowledge culture (but what we might call fandom) and was perhaps the first transmedia franchise to successfully incorporate the energy feeding back from its audience, who were not only passively or even cooperatively absorbing the media products of a huge, faceless corporation, but were working together to *produce* content that served as paratext for the universe they shared across their minds. As Jenkins points out, Star Wars was among the first corporate entertainment products to take advantage not only of the newly emerging technological possibilities for interactivity (enabling user feedback) and participation (encouraging or at least not attempting to shut down unauthorized but enthusiastic media production based on their intellectual property). There was a somewhat porous boundary between fandom and the so-called Expanded Universe of the Star Wars novels, games, etc., where participation in the universe and communication with the Powers That Be (George Lucas and the various authors contracted to write Star Wars novels and comics and so on) gave fans a feeling of being a collective. Whether or not it was accurate is somewhat beside the point. Star Wars fan films helped a number of people break into the industry. Before the internet was a major force for communication, unofficial Star Wars fanzines and even the letter columns in officially licensed Star Wars comics created communities that included both fans and creators, and not infrequently saw one turn into the other and back again.

Both Star Wars and Ninja Turtles were (and are) major cultural phenomena based on original works that led into transmedia narratives and multi-billion dollar merchandising successes. Both are strongly rooted in pastiche and nostalgia, but both are also enjoyable on their own merits without any prior knowledge of the texts to which they pay homage. But Ninja Turtles, I think, inhabits and deploys convergence culture in an even more profound and influential way.

In the first place, it helped that Ninja Turtles was always more accessible than Star Wars. This was largely a matter of pure technological availability: if you bought the original

TMNT comic, you had it forever and could read it as many times as you pleased. Whereas if you wanted to see *Star Wars* again, you'd have to go buy another movie ticket — it would be years before VCRs made the original movies objects that you could legitimately own and re-experience at your leisure. This was one reason that the *Star Wars* action figures were such an unexpectedly big hit (and why George Lucas's true genius lies in his trading his financial stake in the movies for royalties from merchandising, as part of his deal for getting the first film made) — you could go home and play *Star Wars* with them — but that didn't give them any inherent advantage over the myriad action figures from all the other properties that followed, including TMNT.

Star Wars (as Henry Jenkins correctly points out) definitely spurred a generation of creative fanaticism that made its way back to George Lucas's Skywalker Ranch, but at the end of the day George Lucas was on *that* side of the screen and you were stuck on *this* one. *Star Wars* was still a special-effects heavy, massively expensive corporate product owned by Universal Studios. You could hope to get a job directing movies someday, but you couldn't make them all by yourself and become successful as an artist that way. The technology to make professional-quality movies without a Hollywood studio and an astronomical budget didn't yet exist. Comics were the same — Batman was great, and maybe you could create some cool superhero and make a living writing comics, but you'd have to work for Marvel or DC and sign away your rights; there just wasn't another way to do it. The flow of creative energy was still, for the most part, one way, because the means of production were 100 percent in the hands of corporations. The necessary technology to produce comic books independently plus the media framework that allowed cultural products to proliferate were available for anyone to use when Eastman and Laird created the Turtles, but the fact is that no one else did it until they did. Technological convergence, plus the punk rock DIY attitude of the 1980s, plus genuine passion and creativity was a powerful alchemy that made new things possible. Eastman and Laird were pioneers in the creator's rights movement that transformed the political economy of the transmedia franchise in a way that George Lucas, with all his creative control, never came close to doing. The indie model leveled the playing field, reclaiming a large proportion of the power that corporate media had usurped from creators, radically reforming the architecture of production from both the artists' and media's sides of things. There was a revolution in the business model of media, from creative products being entirely commissioned, financed, and owned by corporations to a *licensing* system, where creators could make their own rules, maintain their rights, make a living off their art without having to sell their souls, and find artistic *and* financial success. Never before could an artist become a billionaire by drawing cartoons in the kitchen.

This was entirely the result of Ninja Turtles and the completely original strategy of Surge Licensing, the fledgling company founded in 1986 that "discovered," developed, and marketed an obscure but brilliant indie comic, saw its potential, and turned it into a global and enduring transmedia sensation. *Ninja Turtles* broke the system that had kept creators apart from fans — as cordial a relationship as George Lucas frequently had with his fans, it was always still arm's length. A fan had to become part of the system before his or her *Star Wars*–influenced creative contributions could be legitimized. The success of *Ninja Turtles*, on the other hand, made *Ninja Turtles* fans aware of the existence of an alternative venue for creation and distribution that could put anyone instantly on even ground (at least in terms of the means of production) with Eastman and Laird themselves. TMNT didn't invent independent culture, of course, but it did turn the underground into the merely *alternative*, granting legitimacy and the potential for commercial and artistic success to those who had never had it before. It was like giving out free superpowers; everything from Jeff Smith's *Bone* to Daniel Clowes's *Eightball* and beyond can trace its success to the trail blazed by *TMNT Volume 1*.

TMNT also created the model for the effective use of nostalgia as a combination storytelling and marketing tool (as opposed to nostalgia for its own sake), and we can see its effects in the comparable transmedia franchises today. The Star Wars Expanded Universe could have served as a template for later transmedia franchises where nostalgia was one of the primary engines of commercial appeal and selling toys was another; but, in fact, what we see is that cartoons that followed the Star Wars pattern for adaptation failed, whereas those that followed the TMNT pattern succeeded.

Star Wars spawned two canonical cartoons in the

mid-1980s; *Star Wars: Ewoks* ran for two seasons and 35 episodes between 1985 and 1986, and *Droids* only ran for 13 episodes during the same time period. The first Turtles series, in comparison, ran for ten years and was ubiquitous in syndication. Hundreds of Star Wars novels appeared, but they had much more niche appeal. The Turtles' success could be shrugged off by insisting that the Ninja Turtles cartoon lasted ten years *because* it was successful, not that it was successful because the franchise was all over the place, unlike *Ewoks* and *Droids* in the case of Star Wars. The success of *Ninja Turtles* was so much greater than that of *Ewoks* and *Droids* because the Star Wars cartoons weren't much more than toy commercials rather than genuine storytelling vehicles. *Ninja Turtles* was also, undeniably, a toy commercial. But it was *also* a relatable narrative that was true to the spirit and the dominant tropes of its inspiring work. Comparatively, *Ewoks* and *Droids* were fan fiction (albeit canonical fan fiction), without any of the archetypal or pastiche elements that made the Star Wars movies so compelling. The mainstream transmedia narrative adaptations of Star Wars that premiered before TMNT remodeled the landscape were significant artistic failures.

To illustrate the difference, let's take He-Man and My Little Pony, a pair of typical 1980s pre-TMNT toy-commercial-style media products. We remember both of these — the cartoons and the toys — and I think it's safe to say that they are equivalent properties that targeted their respective audience quadrants with more or less the same strategy. *He-Man and the Masters of the Universe* and *My Little Pony* both lasted only two seasons each. Yet they made an indelible impression and their nostalgia power is considerable. Now, when Mattel (owner of He-Man) and Hasbro (owner of My Little Pony) got smart and relaunched the franchises (in 2002 and 2010, respectively) to capitalize on the 21st century nostalgia boom, they did so in very different ways.

The new *He-Man and the Masters of the Universe* was superior to the original in terms of writing, animation, and continuity, and included all the requisite nods to its predecessors. Yet it only lasted two seasons and was generally a failure both artistically and commercially. Its mistake was following the Star Wars transmedia model (that is, what *Ewoks* and *Droids* and, Force help us all, the *Star Wars Holiday Special* did): it relied on pure nostalgia as fuel. That works if you're selling t-shirts; it does *not* work for narrative media.

My Little Pony is a whole other story. Animator Lauren Faust was selected as showrunner for the relaunched series *My Little Pony: Friendship Is Magic*, and she very much followed the Ninja Turtles model (whether consciously or not) in her adaptation — the model created by the original Turtles cartoon as well as the 2003 series that succeeded in returning the Turtles to the media stage. Faust deeply understood the strengths and weaknesses of *My Little Pony* and knew that she couldn't rely purely on nostalgia if she wanted the show to succeed *as a show*. Faust's *My Little Pony* is deeply intertextual, respectful of its origins, not afraid to diverge when it makes sense to do so but never changing things simply for the sake of changing them. It is funny, culturally aware, and relevant, with a complex yet solid moral core. And it succeeded in a *major* way. It even managed to hit all four quadrants (young and old, male and female) the way that Ninja Turtles in its many incarnations did and continues to do.

The creative models pioneered by TMNT, which catalyzed convergence culture in a way that not even Star Wars could do, continue to work, and not only for adaptations. *Adventure Time*, created by Pendleton Ward and running on Cartoon Network since 2010, does exactly the same thing, and it's brilliant because of it. It's profoundly intertextual while never resorting to ripping off other works; it's absolutely steeped in nostalgia[55] but never overly relies on it for cheap appeal; it's funny and weird in a sophisticated way and has a complex, realistic morality that problematizes and yet ultimately reinforces itself. In other words, it has an extremely sophisticated reader model. And this has translated very well into *Adventure Time*'s various adaptations, precisely the way that TMNT did before it — for instance, the Eisner Award–winning comic book, published by BOOM! Studios and written by illustrious web cartoonist Ryan North.

There's a huge amount of groundbreaking originality in both *My Little Pony: Friendship Is Magic* and *Adventure Time*, two transmedia franchises at the forefront of today's culture, but

---

55 *Adventure Time* is set in a world 1,000 years in the future, after a cataclysm called the Great Mushroom War destroyed civilization and unleashed the power of magic across the devastated Earth. Its protagonist, the barely adolescent Finn, is the last human in a world now populated by talking dogs, anthropomorphic candy, wizards, vampires, and basically anything else you can think of — and he displays very believably conflicting feelings about his place and the meaning of his life. That sets a certain wistful tone that permeates the show, but doesn't weigh it down or overshadow the humor or the storyline.

both of them are located squarely in the artistic and commercial space first conquered by Teenage Mutant Ninja Turtles.

With new comics and the prestige republication of the original Eastman and Laird books, with a new and very popular cartoon, and the increasing availability of previous animated versions of the Turtles for older fans and new ones alike, with a new movie dragging the property back into high-profile controversy, not to mention new TMNT videogames, TMNT action figures, TMNT sneakers and TMNT birthday cake toppers, we're clearly in a resurgence. We've already examined why it's unlikely that this will be one of those flash-in-the-pan things that burn bright for a little while and then flame out. The return of TMNT isn't fueled purely by nostalgia, as we've seen. There are new ideas at the forefront of the reinvigorated Turtles media, and it's attracting an entirely new generation of fans for at least the third time in as many decades (depending on how exactly you want to count) — kids who were not born when the original comic came out, or when the first cartoon came out, and who may not even have been born when the *second series* culminated with *Turtles Forever*! The themes and tropes that make the Turtleverse tick, and the characters and sensibility that are the engine of its progress, clearly are rooted somewhere deep in the collective unconscious of postmodernity; that alone should be enough to ensure that the Turtles have a lot of fertile territory yet to explore in every medium — as long as they're helmed by creative people who understand

and care about the characters. Mutability is an essential piece of the Turtles' appeal, and structurally the capacity for diverse storytelling and deep reimagining is a large part of what made them so popular in the first place. New Turtles series, entire new Turtles universes, shouldn't be feared but embraced when they live up to the quality of what's come before and when they honor and engage with the deep questions that make the Turtles as culturally relevant today as they have been in the past.

Finally, a wish list for this latest cycle of the evolution and rebirth of Teenage Mutant Ninja Turtles.

Obviously we all want Eastman and Laird to reunite. They're the Lennon and McCartney of indie comics — strong enough on their own, but unstoppable, if pugnacious, when together. When they reformed after years of working apart for the "Return to New York" storyline, it was the best stuff that Turtles fans had seen since the original comic's long first run of no-hitters. When they did it again for the incredibly ambitious 13-part "City at War," the magic was there too, with strong new characters, distinctive personalities shining through from all our favorites, philosophical depth, and kickassingly brutal ninja action all in perfect proportion. It's been a very long time since then, but if their most recent individual work is any indication, both of them are still at the top of their game when they're motivated to be, their personal artistic strengths still precisely well balanced to harmonize with the other's. Very yin and yang.

That said, I also really hope to see the conclusion of *TMNT*

Volume 4. Some very major threads were left hanging when Peter Laird sold the property to Nickelodeon, and it would be a shame if the original Mirage canon were to leave off in such an ambiguous place, with the Turtles spread out through space and dimensions, contending with new and frightening changes to themselves and their world, alone. I want to see what happens, and I want it to be the genuine canon, straight from the creators' minds.

The time also seems right for an anthology series like Mirage's old *Turtle Soup*. Maybe in the vein of Marvel's *Strange Tales*. Let's give some of today's best writers and artists their shot at re-envisioning the Turtles their way. What would Robert Kirkman's TMNT be like? Or Mark Waid's? Matt Fraction's? What would the *Penny Arcade* guys do with the Turtles? Bryan Lee O'Malley? Or maybe even Frank Miller? Imagine a TMNT/Daredevil crossover! That would be in the spirit of intertextuality that gave birth to the Turtles in the first place, as well as the participatory experimentation that made the series a touchstone for indie creators. How many of today's creative bigshots would credit TMNT with having showed them how it could be done?

What else? A Turtles RPG videogame would be pretty awesome. There have been a lot of Turtles games, including many good ones, but almost all of them have been fighters or side-scrolling beat-em-ups. The new generation of Turtles game has already begun — the infinite-runner style game *Rooftop Run* for iOS and the third-person brawler *Out of the Shadows* on Steam/Xbox Live/PlayStation Network, built on Epic Games's *Unreal*

Engine, are both fun and charming in their own ways — but a Ninja Turtles game with the storytelling depth of which RPGs are capable could be a triumph like *Planescape: Torment, Knights of the Old Republic, Dragon Age, Bioshock*, or even the Final Fantasy series of games, where immersive worlds and well-defined characters create compelling and meaningful gameplay. It's a natural evolution of the tabletop roleplaying game that was the very first TMNT adaptation of all; technology is finally catching up to where pencils and 20-sided dice have been for decades. In the true indie spirit, it would allow players to participate actively in the unfolding narrative rather than just absorb it.

And believe it or not, there's never been an adaptation that had the same level of grit and grimness as the original comic book. It would be fantastic to try out an R-rated TMNT thing, one that was decidedly not for kids. Think of Zack Snyder's adaptation of *Watchmen* — whatever your opinion of that film, it certainly attempted something that other superhero movies hadn't before, and a TMNT film could easily inhabit a similar space. Or maybe an animated series (or miniseries? Direct-to-DVD or Netflix?) à la Genndy Tartakovsky's *Samurai Jack*. That style would suit the Turtles excellently — after all, one of TMNT's greatest strengths is its intrinsic versatility, so why use it for exclusively PG-rated, family-friendly fare?

There's just so much possibility. So many angles to examine and stories left to tell. Take Batman. Batman has been through a lot. He first emerged in May 1939, into a civilization months shy of the first World Science Fiction Convention and the Second World War — really think about that. When Batman began, there was no *Star Trek* or Auschwitz. If that sounds crass, it's not intended to be; it's just meant to show that this planet was a very, *very* different place then. In some ways more innocent and naïve, and much more primitive and unsubtle in others. But people back then related to Batman just as we relate to him now. Someone born today could easily be a fourth-generation Batman fan in just a couple of years. In contrast, nobody in the world has great-grandparents who were, say, Scientologists. So Batman transcends the generations, and yet today's Batman is very different from yesterday's. His rogues gallery consists of hundreds of characters, and he's gone through nearly that many Robins. He's also died and returned about a dozen times, proving that sometimes even what does kill you makes you stronger. But even more impressive than coming back from the grave is coming back from ignominious bullshit; the slapstick absurdity of the 1960s Adam West television series, the poorly animated and embarrassingly emasculated *Super Friends* cartoon, and the utterly rotten *Batman & Robin* movie came frighteningly close to gutting the franchise and turning the Caped Crusader into a bad joke that even the Riddler wouldn't have deigned to utter.

And yet that's not what happened. The Dark Knight always rises again. I think it was Neil Gaiman who said that Batman is stronger and better than any individual Batman story. Something about that character, his identity/ies, his motivations, his modus operandi, speaks to us and gives Batman an immunity to being ephemeral and disposable like so much other stuff in our culture.

Teenage Mutant Ninja Turtles, I think it's safe to say, possesses the same kind of tenacity. The world into which the Turtles first hatched was quite different than the one in which we live today. Forty-five years to the month after the first appearance of Batman in *Detective Comics* #27, *TMNT* #1 was published. The world was on the brink of the unexpected end to the Cold War, sending the political and economic realities of the past half-century into upheaval. It was also the dawn of independent publishing's radical ascendancy, and of global electronic communications significantly leveling the playing field for creators and consumers alike. The Turtles, just like Batman, have also had some serious missteps throughout their history — that cheap third movie, the whole late '90s debacle, and even, arguably, the first cartoon which could have watered down the hard-hitting disposition of the property so far beyond recognition that it might never have recovered. And yet that's not what happened. TMNT endured the inevitable indignities and failures and emerged from the other side triumphant, with a few lessons learned and important new skills for survival gained. We're in a good place for the moment, Turtle-wise, and I think that TMNT will continue on in the same way. Batman has been around for 70 years and is as strong as he's ever been; the ever-youthful TMNT are only just beginning their fourth decade.

There's a giant tortoise named Jonathan living on the South Atlantic island of Saint Helena who's thought to have been born around 1832 — same year, incidentally, as Lewis Carroll (creator of another particularly unconventional reptile, as a matter of fact, the melancholy Mock Turtle) — possibly making Jonathan the world's oldest living animal. And the Teenage Mutant Ninja Turtles could easily find themselves similarly perennial. TMNT's future may include mistakes and setbacks — certainly *will* include mistakes and setbacks — but these could never be fatal. What are turtles known for if not their profound longevity and their hard-shelled resilience? And what is a mutant's greatest advantage, if not the endless capacity for adaptation, the uncanny ability to thrive in new and difficult circumstances? When it comes right down to it, isn't that what Turtle Power is all about?

*Notes

The quote from Ovid's *Metamorphoses* is from the translation by Brookes More (Boston: Cornhill Publishing, 1922).

The information on crime statistics in New York comes from "Uniform Crime Reports and Index of Crime in New York in the State of New York enforced by New York City from 1985 to 2005" (http://www.disastercenter.com/newyork/crime/9004.htm).

Marvel's argument that mutants are not humans for import tax purposes is from *Toy Biz v. United States* (United States Court of International Trade January 3, 2003).

The quoted passage by Roger Ebert comes from his review of *Teenage Mutant Ninja Turtles II: The Secret of the Ooze* in *I Hated, Hated, Hated This Movie* (Kansas City, MO: Andrews McMeel Publishing, 2000).

The *Hollywood Reporter* press release on the sale of *TMNT* to Nickelodeon is by Georg Szalai. ("Ninja Turtles snapped up by Nickelodeon." Reuters. Web. October 21, 2009. http://www.reuters.com/article/2009/10/22/us-ninja-idUSTRE59L01520091022).

Acknowledgments

Thanks to The One-Above-All;[56] my parents, for indulging my obsession all these years, and my friends, for sharing it with me; Jen Knoch and Crissy Calhoun, for believing in this book and for their invaluable help, astute observations and improvements on every page, and their ceaseless enthusiasm each step of the way; Hal Niedzviecki, without whom it is very likely that my writing aspirations would be precisely nowhere today, and my gratitude to whom is correspondingly eternal; Emma Healey, for so much more than support; the whole crew of OverthinkingIt.com, the website that subjects the popular culture to a level of scrutiny it probably doesn't deserve; everyone at *Broken Pencil* magazine; Susi Mazzotta, for *TMNT Volume 1* #1; Erin Creasey, Sarah Dunn, Michelle Melski, and everyone at ECW Press; TVtropes.com;[57] and, of course, Kevin Eastman and Peter Laird, and everyone from Mirage Studios, who have inspired and enriched generations. *Turtles Forever!*

---

56 See *Sensational Spider-Man Volume 2* #40, True Believers!

57 Warning: TVtropes.

Richard Rosenbaum is a fiction editor at *Broken Pencil* (Canada's magazine of the underground arts and independent culture) and a regular contributor to OverthinkingIt.com. He has a Master's degree in communication and culture, and this is what he's doing with it. He lives in Toronto, Ontario. His favourite Turtle is Donatello.

At ECW Press, we want you to enjoy this book in whatever
format you like, whenever you like. Leave your print book
at home and take the eBook to go! Purchase the print
edition and receive the eBook free. Just send an email to
ebook@ecwpress.com and include:

- the book title
- the name of the store where you purchased it
- your receipt number
- your preference of file type: PDF or ePub?

A real person will respond to your email with your eBook
attached. And thanks for supporting an independently
owned Canadian publisher with your purchase!